Frank Rutherford

French Housing, Laws & Taxes

Fifth Edition

SPRUCEHURST LTD

25 Vanston Place
London SW6 1AZ

First published 1979
Fifth revised edition published 1995
© Frank Rutherford 1979, 1985, 1986, 1990, 1995

Whilst the advice and information in this book is believed to be true and accurate at the time of going to press, neither the author nor the publisher can accept any legal responsibility for any error or omissions that may occur.

All rights reserved. No reproduction, copy or transmission of this publication may be made without written permission.
No paragraph of this publication may be reproduced, copies or transmitted save with written permission or in accordance with the provision of the Copyright Act 1956 (as amended). Any person who does any unauthorised act in relation to this publication may be liable to criminal prosecution and civil claims for damages.

ISBN : 09515226 0 4

Printed and bound in Great Britain by
Biddles Ltd, Guildford and King's Lynn

CONTENTS

PREFACE TO FIFTH EDITION

The number of persons, British and otherwise, who have bought properties in France has expanded enormously since the last edition of this book. Most have interesting stories to tell, and I am sure that all have felt the experience of owning a piece of France to have been an enriching one. None of these owners can have failed to enjoy the renowned French quality of life, and for North Europeans in particular the benign climate has health giving qualities.

Buying a French property, whether for holidays, retirement or investment, requires planning, some shrewd decision making and above all information. This is what I endeavour, as always, to supply with this book. Information of a practical kind, with some down-to-earth tips, pointers to the golden rules, and warnings of the pitfalls to avoid.

In this edition I have extended the information to include matters of interest to nationals of countries other than Great Britain. In the first place I have tried to take into account the needs of all English-speaking countries, but also to include our friends in other parts of Europe who are prepared pursue the French life-style by reading this book in English. There are occasions, however, when I have been unable to avoid to specific references to Britain and for this I apologise to non-British readers.

Those who plan to live in France and earn a living by running a business, even part-time, will be interested in the new chapter on Setting up in Business. This is an area where information, and the correct information at that, is vital. Many matters have to be taken into consideration: taxation, business structure, rules and regulations. This is an area where it is easy when you know how, but the whole exercise can appear quite daunting to a novice.

I hope that this book will assist you in your search and to guide you through the transaction to a successful conclusion.

Frank Rutherford

1. INTRODUCTION - WHERE TO BUY AND HOW TO CHOOSE

Many people know in advance where they want to go in France. This is because they will have spent holidays already in a favourite locality - probably in a *gite*. Once a liking for a particular spot has been established, and friends made locally, it makes sense to go back to the same place. Deciding where to buy then becomes easy.

Many others, however, have no idea where they want to buy and this chapter will endeavour to shed some light on the different options, and highlight the advantages and disadvantages of the different regions of France. It will also give a tip or two about where the smart money is going.

As a very general rule, there is a trade-off in France between accessibility and climate. The Northern part is very accessible to visitors from Britain, but naturally the further south one goes the hotter and sunnier the climate becomes.

They say that the Loire Valley is the dividing line and it is astonishing how, as one drives south, the clouds seem to part and the sun shines hotter just as one crosses the river at Tours or Saumur.

Not that the weather need be at all bad in northern France. In fact, the sun has a much stronger "bite" to it anywhere in Normandy than at home. In Brittany, many an Anglo-Saxon holiday maker has underestimated the sun's strength. Even a lightly cloudy sky can bring a sunburn.

One reason for this is the Atlantic seaboard location. All of Brittany and Normandy is influenced by the Atlantic. This brings with it variable conditions, but the sunny intervals are witness to very clear air. Photographers love the sharpness of the light and the brilliant colours that the climate bestows. Only on the west coast of Ireland have I seen the same.

Some people prefer northern France because they, or their young children, do not like car journeys. It is true that all parts north of the Loire can be reached in under four hours of the Western channel ports. After an overnight ferry crossing, one can be on the road by 8am and in one's house well before lunchtime.

But for many, there is the desire to go south; further south to where the sun blazes out of a cloudless sky; to where the heat drives man and beast into the shade. This is a different France with a more latin and meridional atmosphere. The architecture changes too, and you can tell by observing the roofs of the houses. As soon as you reach the Charente, the roof pitch becomes shallower and the tiles are of the rounded "over and under" type, commonly known as Roman tiles. These were used over two thousand years ago in Ancient Rome and the design has not changed since.

The whole south west of France is accepted by visitors as an excellent compromise between southerly climate and accessibility. If one goes further into the deep south of the Languedoc or Provence, the extra journey time takes you away from the green landscape of the Dordogne and the Lot and into a harsher and more arid world. The ability of the south west to stay green in high summer is universally appreciated.

And yet the Mediterranean hinterland succeeds in seducing many people with its magic. Hill-top villages stand guard over vineyards and scrub over which clings the scent of tarragon, thyme and rosemary.

The hills of the Languedoc and Provence have borne witness to many human conflicts. The Greeks came first, although they kept to the coastline, then the Romans. After the fall of Rome came the Vandals, Franks and Saxons from the north and Moors from the south. A lot of blood was shed and that is why the villages are all perched up on high ground for safety. The narrow streets and ramparts all contribute to the special atmosphere.

The village houses, however, that are clustered together cheek by jowl, do have a disadvantage for modern housebuyers. They usually lack any type of garden, but on the other hand they have breath-taking views from the upper terraces.

At the end of the day, it is one's budget that largely determines the matter. If one cannot afford Provence, a perfectly acceptable alternative is the Languedoc which has the same feel and climate, but at lower cost. Another alternative to Provence is the Ardèche, just to the north. It is beautiful and rugged, and the summers enjoy the same glorious temperatures.

For many, the western side of France has been a favourite. It is inexpensive, unspoilt and easy to get to. For those who find that the Dordogne contains too many British, then there are alternatives nearby. The Corrèze is one, as is the Limousin around Limoges (where limousine carriages came from). They are cheaper too.

Other alternatives are the Gers, west of Toulouse, and the Tarn, east of Toulouse. The scenery gets wilder as one goes further east and south. When you end up in the Lozère, you find yourself in the least populated area of all (the Lozère phone book is as thin as a Sunday colour supplement).

For those who want to stay closer to home, there is of course Normandy. It is a vast region, comprising five *départements* and an area as big as Hampshire, Sussex, Surrey and Kent put together. Parts of Normandy, to the east, are quite close to Paris and in consequence more expensive. Deauville is no bargain basement either. But if one goes west to the Manche or south into the Orne, then prices tumble.

The further one goes up the northern coast towards Calais the closer one gets to home and the more accessible are the properties. Visiting the house just for the weekend then becomes a feasible proposition. The Channel Tunnel serves the *départements* of Pas-de-Calais, Somme and at a pinch the Seine Maritime. Anything further afield would increase the driving time and shorten the weekend enjoyment.

When all is said and done, the choice has to be a subjective one. One must weigh up the different options. A cheap unmodernised cottage will require renovation. Some people find this all part of the fun, others are daunted by the prospect of controlling builders at long distance. Buying a country property that has been modernised, or at least in part, may be more acceptable. Naturally the cost would be higher but with less to spend later, if anything. Many British buyers however find that some properties have been over-converted, and it is true that many local French owners modernise old properties to such an extent that a lot of the old charm has been lost. In these cases one would also be paying for costly "improvements" that are unwelcome.

A large number of people who wish to put all these matters to one side prefer to buy new, either a house or an apartment. These properties are more often than not purchased off-plan. They need not be confined to the well known coastal resorts but can be chalets or ski flats in the Alps or even new country properties in traditional rural areas. These can be a good compromise between tradition and convenience.

There are some British buyers who would go anywhere provided there are no other British around. The local French are amused by this trait of some of us to shun our fellow *compatriotes*. In a sense it is a compliment to the locals since it is *their* company and life-style that is being sought and not the gin-and-tonic culture from back home.

Whatever one's motive and budget, there is always a warm welcome in France for the overseas buyer, especially if an effort is made to integrate with the local community.

2. CONVEYANCING IN FRANCE

The basic principles

There are two factors which in theory simplify the transfer of title in France. First, all freehold title is registered; secondly, the conveyance is performed by only one lawyer, the notary (*notaire*), who acts independently of both parties as an impartial official.

The Land Registry (*cadastre*) maintains a map showing land split into sections (*parcelles*) each numbered and showing the surface area and use to which it is put, eg dwelling house, agricultural building, meadow, vineyard, etc. The Land Registry works in conjunction with the *Conservation des Hypothèques* which maintains a register of all mortgages and other charges which affect the title. In this way, it is relatively easy to ascertain beforehand exactly what the position is regarding title.

In Britain and America, where an adversarial legal system operates, it is customary for the vendor and purchaser each to be represented by his own solicitor or attorney. In France this is unnecessary, as the legal function is carried out by the independent notaire who draws up the contract (*acte*), witnesses the signatures, collects and disburses the purchase price and registers the transfer.

The choice of notaire is usually in the hands of the vendor who will appoint the local man who already has the property on file. The purchaser is entitled to appoint his own notaire if he wishes, but it is important to realise that the two practitioners will not act in opposition to each other as solicitors do in England, but *jointly*. Since the joint notaires have to split the statutory fee, they are not always too happy about this arrangement.

The final deed of sale has to be signed in the notaire's office itself. If the vendor or purchaser live far away or cannot attend for any reason, the notaire will draw up a power of attorney to allow someone else to sign instead. In many cases the notaire's clerk acts as proxy and his name is sometimes not inserted in the power of attorney until the last minute, depending on which of the clerks is free at the time of signature.

Various formalities may have to be attended to, which can complicate the basic simplicity of the system. For example, if the property to be sold has to be detached from a larger estate, or if an existing *parcelle* is to be split in two, a land surveyor *(géomètre)* must draw up a site plan which has to be registered beforehand with the *cadastre*. If the property is situated in a rural zone and the land area is over a certain size the French Land Commission *(S.A.F.E.R.)* has to give prior approval of the sale. The agency was set up by the French Government to organise the consolidation of farms into less fragmented and more efficient units. It has the power of pre-emption on all rural sales but now rarely exercises it, except where an important piece of agricutural land is involved.

All monies should be paid to the notaire, or estate agent licensed to hold clients' deposits, who will hold the funds as stakeholder pending completion. French notaires are bonded, so clients are protected in the event of misfeasance or other irregularity whilst clients' money is in their hands. If both purchaser and vendor are non-residents of France, it is possible in most cases for the price to be paid direct from one to the other in another currency. In such cases a stakeholder has to be appointed in their own country, usually the vendor's solicitor or both acting jointly.

Unless special arrangements are made otherwise, the signing of the final deed and completion will be simultaneous. This is because, whereas in England a contract is signed first and its implementation carried out afterwards (completion), in France it is the other way around. The price is paid first and the details attended to prior to signature, so that when the deed is finally signed, the purchaser at that moment becomes legal owner.

He will not however receive his copy of the deed until it has been stamped at the Land Registry and returned to the notaire's office about two months later. Notaires usually prefer to hand the deed over to the purchaser personally rather than send it through the post. It should be remembered that there is not a Title Deed as such. Possession of the final deed is in itself not proof of ownership - this is provided and guaranteed by the Land Registry.

It should be remembered that the notaire is an independent official who operates at arms length from both vendor and purchaser. He cannot be asked to perform tasks such as requesting the vendor to arrange for electricity to be connected, or asking him to clear out his barn, etc. Such duties should be performed by the estate agent. (In some parts of France, notaires act as estate agents too and receive commission on top of their legal fees. These chores can in this event be asked of them. Whether ot not they will perform them with alacrity is another matter).

3. BUYING A PROPERTY IN FRANCE

The Procedure Step-by-Step
So you have chosen a property and you declare your intention to go ahead. You must remember that from this point on your legal standing will be quite different from what you may be used to at home. Whereas in Great Britain (Scotland excepted) you can always proceed "subject to contract", in France (as in Spain and Italy) you will be asked to sign a preliminary agreement and pay a deposit. This is the point of no return.

In fact it is a good and workable system, and it cuts out much of the uncertainty of other systems. This is how you proceed.

EXISTING PROPERTIES

The Deposit
The deposit *(acompte* or *dépôt de garantie)* will give proof of your *bona fide* intention to purchase. It should never be paid direct to the vendor, since you would have no protection if the vendor were to abscond, or if the property were heavily mortgaged and he failed to put the money towards redeeming the charge. The notaire, or estate agent licensed to hold clients funds, is the person qualified and trusted to hold money as stakeholder. In this way the deposit stays in safe neutral hands pending completion of the transaction.

When you have selected a property, you may be expected to pay a deposit there and then, and to sign a preliminary contract. If the market is active and you fear that a rival buyer might step in, then you should proceed accordingly. On the other hand, the atmosphere may be relaxed and no such pressure applied. Here then are the different alternative courses you can take at this critical point in the transaction:
a) You wish to clinch the deal on the spot; you sign the preliminary contract and pay the deposit.
b) You are more cautious and/or the locals do not put pressure on you; you declare your intention to proceed and ask for the preliminary contract to be sent to your home address for you to sign and send back

with the deposit on your return.

c) A good compromise is to sign the preliminary contract, but to state that the deposit will be sent once you have returned home. However, the contract will be incomplete until the deposit is received and there is a risk that the vendor might change his mind in the meantime, although it is reasonable to assume that he will allow you sufficient time to transfer the funds.

d) It is possible that you are asked to pay a deposit on the spot and to wait for the contract to be sent to you for signature later. This can often happen if the notaire is acting as agent and he wants to be assured of your intention before taking the trouble to draw up a preliminary document. This course is not advisable, since the terms on which the deposit will be held are undetermined and your ability to retrieve it uncertain. If, when you eventually receive the contract, you find it unsatisfactory or some matters come to light that were not brought to your attention originally, you may wish to withdraw and claim back the deposit. For example, there may be a right of way through your property in favour of a neighbouring farmer. Since you may be reluctant to have your evening *apéritif* disturbed by his tractor weaving its way through your newly planted garden, you decide to cancel and request a refund of the deposit. You will have no guarantee that the other side will comply.

The Preliminary Contract
This agreement is given a variety of names in French (*compromis de vente, promesse de vente* and *sous-seing privé*). The various types have subtle differences which I shall not go into here. Instead, we shall concentrate on the terms that they should contain, especially in respect of the deposit.

The preliminary contract is a private document and not a notarised deed (although the notaire will often be the one to draw it up). Its purpose is to set out the outlines of the transaction; in effect it is an agreement to agree. Its advantage is that the price of the property is fixed, cutting out the fear of "gazumping". Also the parties are committed up to a point, eliminating uncertainties.

The Terms of the Preliminary Contract
This document should always set out the following:

1. Full **identification of the parties** involved. This is particularly important in the case of vendors who may comprise several members of the same family, owning the property jointly.

2. Proper legal **identification of the property**. It is surprising how many times a property is merely described as a house situated in the

parish *(commune)* of X village. The parties of course know which house they are talking of, but legally it could be any one of a number of properties.

3. A declaration by the vendor that the property is to be sold with **vacant possession** and is **free of easements** (such as rights of way, etc).

4. An agreement by the vendor to sell and by the purchaser to buy at a given price.

5. The amount of deposit is then stated, usually 10%, together with the name of the stakeholder *(séquestre)*, normally the estate agent provided he is licensed and bonded.

6. The terms on which the deposit is held. The purchaser will traditionally lose the deposit if he backs out of the deal for a reason not provided for in the contract (see "let-out" clauses below). The vendor should be committed to the transaction either way, although sometimes he is given the option to back out on payment of a sum equal to the deposit, as indemnity to the purchaser, who of course also gets the original deposit back. Occasionally the contract is drafted in such a way that if the vendor withdraws, the purchaser has to sue for specific performance, but this can be a problem if it also involves sueing for cancellation of the vendor's sale to another purchaser.

7. **"Let-out" clauses** *(clauses suspensives)*. There are three such clauses that are usually standard.

(a) Non-availability of mortgage finance. Consumer legislation in France allows a prospective purchaser to withdraw from such a contract if he is unable to obtain a mortgage or other loan destined for the purchase. If it is to be a cash purchase, however, then he will be asked to waive his rights in this respect.

(b) Pre-emption by the S.A.F.E.R. (French Land Commission). In rural areas any property with land may be snapped up by this government agency when it comes on the market. The purpose is to rationalise local agriculture by merging farms, but in the case of small amounts of land (under 2 hectares - 5 acres) the danger of pre-emption is negligible.

(c) Unsatisfactory local planning search. This will come in the form of a document issued by the local planning authority. The notaire will arrange for this and it will come in one of two forms - a *note de renseignements d'urbanisme* which sets out the outline planning situation, or a *certificat d'urbanisme* which is in response to a specific request (eg can the barn be converted to residential use? or can I build a granny flat at the back of the house?). If the search shows that there is a material planning restriction, then the purchaser may withdraw without penalty. For further information on this subject, see Chapter 4.

8. Time limit. The contract traditionally stipulates that completion must take place within two months. However this is usually extended to 2½ months, to allow plenty of time for the S.A.F.E.R. clearance or for the mortgage application to go through. On the other, if all the parties are ready, there is nothing to prevent completion being sooner than the date entered in the contract.

You will early in the proceedings be given a questionnaire and asked a lot of intimate details about your private life. Quite apart from your date of birth (an obsession with the French), you have to state if you are married, single, widowed, separated or divorced. The French for "single" is *célibataire*. Now this means that you are not, *nor never have been* married. Some British buyers living singly after a divorce state that they are single, and this can make a notaire wonder if you have anything to hide. You see, in France your civil status (*état civil*) is sacrosanct and cannot be trifled with. Once committed to the official record, your civil status is immutable. If your were to state your name as Harry when your birth certificate says Henry, you will really make him suspicious.

Even those who are blamessly married have to give explanations. In France, there are two matrimonial *régimes* - that of *communauté* which means joint ownership of all assets, and that of *séparation des biens* whereby spouses own their assets separately. In Great Britain and other Anglo-Saxon countries, all marriages are under the latter *régime* with the difference that the parties do not enter into prenuptial contracts (USA excepted). In France, it is usual for those under *séparation des biens* to provide for the ultimate disposal of their respective assets in a notarised contract.

So, the answer you should give at this stage is that you were married under the régime of *séparation des biens* without a contract. If you give the wrong answers, your executors may have some explaining to do. Do not confuse this issue with that of joint ownership and inheritance, which are dealt with under Chapter 12.

Draft Conveyance Document
During the two month wait, the notaire will prepare the conveyance document (*acte de vente*). A draft copy of this must be requested by the purchaser before completion. It is amazing how many times purchasers are asked to part with the price of a house without this essential safeguard. After all, it is not so much a house that one is buying as title to it and it is the title that is recorded in the document. Without it one may as well buy a pig in a poke.

Some notaires, especially unsophisticated ones in the country, may present a draft with blank spaces in it, which they propose to full in later when the information is to hand. It is essential that the document be complete. Some of the items to look for are:

1. A correct description of yourself and co-purchasers. If husband and wife are buying jointly as tenants in common (*en indivis*) then they will each get 50% of the property, unless instructions are given otherwise. Women are always identified by their maiden names in French legal documents.

2. A correct description of the property. References to the Land Registry parcel numbers (*parcelles cadastrales*) will be supplied. You should obtain a copy of the site plan in order to check that the numbers tally. The notaire or agent wil not always supply this document, since in France it is readily available from the local town hall (*mairie*) and that is where a French purchaser would go to verify that the boundaries of the property match those he was shown on the ground. However this is not always possible for an absentee purchaser, and it is the least the notaire or agent can do to supply you with this essential document.

3. Abstract of title. This explains how the property came into the possession of the vendor.

4. Existence or otherwise of easements. These could be rights of way (not uncommon in the French countryside) and/or restrictive covenants.

5. Confirmation of the planning status of the property. Any French property that falls within a conservation zone will have restrictions on repairs and renewals. This could be because the house falls within a certain radius of an ancient monument such as a chateau or historical church. Sometimes whole villages are subject to these conservation restrictions.

6. The property is unencumbered. That is to say, the vendor has no mortgage or other charge. In fact, if he has, the notaire will redeem the debt out of the sale proceeds before handing over the money to the vendor. This is an important protection afforded the purchaser by the French notarial system.

A sloppy conveyance at this stage can cause problems later at the time of resale or in the event of probate. Unless a purchaser is fully conversant with the French law of property, he should always have a draft conveyance document vetted by a qualified professional.

Completion
Whereas in this country, contracts are signed (exchanged) first and the loose ends sorted out later, in France it is the other way around. The

price is deposited with the notaire first and the other details sorted beforehand, so that at the moment of final signature title chaı hands.

1. On completion the purchaser pays the balance of the purchase price, having already paid a 10% deposit. This is paid to the notaire.

2. The legal charges must also be paid at this stage. These comprise the notaire's fee and the registration tax (roughly equivalent to our stamp duty), all amounting to about 10% for a property worth about 300,000 Frs. The percentage is more for lower prices and less for more expensive ones. If the property has more than 2,500 square metres of land, then the rate on the extra land is charged at a higher rate. The notaire will usually put as low a value as possible on this surplus land in order to keep the tax to a minimum.

3. If a mortgage is taken out on the property, then there will be extra legal charges amounting to about 2-3% of the amount borrowed.

4. If the property is to be detached from a larger estate or if new boundaries have to be drawn, then a land surveyor (*géomètre*) will have to come to the site, measure up and then submit a new site plan to the Land Registry. In these cases it is important to establish who is responsible for his fee, which will amount to approximately 3,000 Frs.

5. When everything is ready, the final conveyance document (*acte de vente*) will be signed. At that moment the property will belong to the purchaser and the money becomes the property of the vendor. This signature must take place in the notaire's office, and since many overseas purchasers do not wish to make a special journey for this purpose, it is possible to grant a power of attorney (*procuration*) to allow someone else to sign on their behalf. Usually the notaire will appoint one of his clerks to perform this task and his name will probably have been left blank until the notaire knows which of his clerks is to be appointed.

6. The conveyance document must then be sent by the notaire to the Land Registry for registration and it will not be available for collection until about two months later. Notaires usually prefer to hand this over personally to the new owner rather than commit it to the post. In any event, it should be remembered that possession of this document is itself no proof of ownership. This is provided by the Land Registry and guaranteed by the state.

BUYING NEW FROM A DEVELOPER
(CONSTRUCTION COMPLETED)

With a new property in a development, the paperwork will be more voluminous than for an individual house on resale. This is partly because the law in France is quite strict in its defence of the co-owners' status and partly because title comprises outright ownership of the apartment or villa plus shared ownership of the common parts (staircase, garden, swimming pool, etc).

In a co-ownership *(copropriété)* - in the USA they call it condominium - a number of statutory measures exist to protect purchasers from the problems that can arise from communal occupancy. In practice, there has to be a deed governing the rules and regulations of the building *(règlement de copropriété)*. In this document all the covenants are listed (as they would in a lease in Britain) and the procedure for the annual general meeting of all the co-owners, selecting a committee and appointing a managing agent. It is a substantial document running sometimes to 100 pages or more.

Co-owners' title is represented in the form of shares in the whole development. Depending on the size of the unit to be purchased, a certain number of one-thousandth or ten-thousandth shares will be allocated together with a further block of shares representing the common parts. The number of shares also determines the voting strength of the owner at the annual general meeting and his share of the service charges.

The procedure is roughly the same as for conventional resales. The deposit will be 10%. The preliminary contract will also need to be signed, although some of the 'let-out' clauses mentioned above will not apply. For example, no certificate of urbanism will be forthcoming (details of the planning approval will form part of the documentation). Similarly, the French Land Commission (SAFER) will not be involved. However, the purchaser will be entitled to withdraw if a mortgage application is refused. If *no* loan is being applied for, then a hand-written declaration has to be made to that effect.

After signature of the preliminary contract, the notaire must still produce a draft copy of the conveyance document for your prior approval. It will be much bulkier than for an individual resale property, since the whole technical history of the development will be incorporated into it, including all the various planning permissions and sub-divisions of the complex.

The vendor must also supply a copy of the *réglement de copropriété* (co-ownership rules) so that you can check the way the development is run and acquaint yourself in advance with the covenants that you will be expected to observe as an occupant. Be that as it may, it is very much a formality since there are rules in France that protect the interests of co-owners and many such documents are produced according to a basic template. However, there can be some nasty surprises that could come to light. For example, the apartment next to yours could turn out to be a doctor's consulting room and your lift and landing subject to a greater flow of visitors than you would wish. (It may interesting to point out here that in France premises used for professional purposes are not deemed to be commercial and can be quite easily mixed in with residential accommodation).

The legal charges for a new building, provided it is not more than five years old, are exempted of registration tax. This will bring the costs down from 10% to about 3%.

BUYING OFF-PLAN FROM A DEVELOPER (UNCOMPLETED CONSTRUCTIONS)

If the development is not yet completed, the sequence of events is changed. The purchaser will be asked to sign a preliminary contract as before but the deposit will be 5% (or 2½% if completion of construction is not scheduled for at least 2 years). Stage payments will then be provided for to be paid as the building progresses. When the final deed is presented for signature, the construction may still not be completed and several stage payments may still have to be made. At this point the purchaser acquires title to the as yet incomplete unit and he can resell it together with its hidden asset value.

It may be that a development is in fact already constructed but that the contract refers to a purchase off-plan. This will occur if the developer is still awaiting a *certificat de conformité* from the local authority and until this is issued, the building will remain classified as uncompleted.

By law, all new developments in France have to be underwritten by a bank, so that if a development company fails before delivery of the property, the purchasers are protected. This is why the deposits for off-plan purchases are made out to the underwriting bank and cannot be used by the developer.

The preliminary contract for a purchase off-plan is called a *contrat de réservation* and the deposit a *dépôt de garantie*. The vendor will be a *réservant* (reserving party) and the purchaser a *réservataire* (beneficiary party). This is because strictly speaking the vendor is not at this stage selling anything (the unit is still not built), but is in fact reserving it for you, the ultimate purchaser.

The purchaser acquires title to the as yet unbuilt apartment

At the same time as signing the preliminary contract you will be asked to sign a copy of the floor plan of your apartment or villa and a copy of the technical specification. In this way you will be protected against any corner-cutting in the standard of construction.

HOW TO PAY FOR YOUR FRENCH PROPERTY

There are three ways in which payment can be made:

1. **Bank draft.** You can instruct your bank at home to issue a draft (cashier's check) in French francs for the required amount drawn up in favour of the notaire. This is a good way to pay if the purchaser is visiting the notaire's office personally and can then hand it over. It is not advisable, however, to send the draft by post, for if it is lost in the

mail, then it is necessary to wait a long time before a new draft can be issued. It is not possible to countermand payment of a draft as with a personal cheque.

2. **Direct transfer** to the notaire's account. This is the quickest method. Your bank will ask you to complete a form giving details of the notaire's account and the money will then be paid directly into it. An 'Urgent' or 'Telegraphic' transfer will take about two to three days. Be sure to state on the form that you will pay the bank charges *at both ends*; otherwise there will be a shortfall in the amount received on the notaire's account.

3. The purchaser can open a **bank account in France** (in fact some notaires insist on this, wrongly). Funds are then transferred to the account and then a cheque drawn in favour of the notaire. This method is slow, mainly because it takes so long to open an account in France and receive a cheque book. It is also a very roundabout way of making what is a straightforward payment.

Naturally in due course you will want to have a French bank account to service your property. When the time comes, I recommend that you do so personally on the spot rather than by correspondence from your home country. It is advisable to select a local bank that is conveniently placed for the property you propose to buy so that money can be drawn out easily when needed.

Having chosen a bank you just walk in and introduce yourself. Opening an account by long distance correspondence will not evoke the same friendly response (in fact you may not even get a reply).

4. PLANNING

In this chapter we shall look at the procedure to be followed in respect of **local searches** and **planning.**

A. Local Searches
In France, the information received from the local searches is less extensive than elsewhere. However, the replies given are quite specific and they are an indispensable part of the purchasing process.

The information comes in the form of a certificate issued by the local planning authority. The request will usually be made by the notaire who is appointed to draw up the conveyance.

If the purchaser has a specific building operation in mind (e.g. construction of a new house, an extension to an existing house, or a change of use such as the conversion of a barn) then he should ask for a *certificat d'urbanisme.* The information contained in this certificate will state whether or not the request is granted and it might also describe the parameters within which the operation must comply. This is a form of outline planning consent.

If no specific building operation is planned, then an abbreviated certificate can be requested, called a *note de renseignements d'urbanisme.* This document will state if there are any planning restrictions or local authority compulsory purchase in the offing. For example, a village house might be situated in a conservation area, due more often than not to its proximity to a ancient church or other historical building. In such cases, listed planning permission must also be sought in the event of external building works.

If the property is situated on a public highway, a certificate defining the status of the road boundaries should also be requested. The document is called an *arrêté d'alignement.* If a road widening scheme is planned by the local or national highway authorities, then the details will be revealed. If the house to be purchased is isolated and accessed by a lone track then there is a case for not bothering with this particular search. But if the property borders on a public thoroughfare, no matter how small or unused, the application should be made. It is quite common for country lanes to be widened or straightened at certain points. This is not done to enable local drivers to hurry home to their lunch (although one could be forgiven for having that impression). The real reason is usually to enable modern combine harvesters to negotiate country lanes that would otherwise be closed to them.

The *certificat d'urbanisme* takes at least two months to obtain and the *note de renseignements d'urbanisme* usually less. If the application is made at the outset, i.e. as soon as the preliminary contract has been signed, then no time will be lost as it also takes this time for the notaire to draw up the conveyance papers.

The road widening certificate is applied for and issued at the same time as the planning certificate.

It is very important that the preliminary contract is made subject to satisfactory planning search. It should contain a let-out clause enabling the purchaser to withdraw without penalty in the event of unacceptable restrictions being revealed by the certificate.

The certificate of urbanism is valid for one year and can be extended for a further twelve months provided application is made at least two months before expiry. Only one extension is permitted.

If a specific building operation is planned, then the specific planning application should be submitted while the *certificat d'urbanisme* is still valid.

B. Planning Permission
The certificate of urbanism provides outline planning permission. Your new house, or extension, can only be built with specific building permission *(permis de construire)*.

If the construction is over 170 m^2 in surface area, or if there is to be an extension to an existing house of over 170 m^2, then the application must be submitted by an architect. Similarly if the applicant is a company, whether limited or not, then an architect must be used irrespective of the size of the operation.

Many purchasers plan merely to modernise an old farmhouse. This may involve opening up new windows and doorways. Such external alterations need building permission and the dimensions of the new openings must comply with certain set rules. Conversion of barns to dwellings require change of use permission if the barns are free standing. A barn that adjoins a house and shares the same roof is deemed to be part of the house itself. Septic tanks also need permission. Work carried out inside the house, however, can be freely undertaken provided it conforms to standard building regulations.

The planning application must be made to the local *mairie* from whom the appropriate forms can be collected. A receipt will be given within two weeks (always called *15 days* in France, while one week is called *8 days*; do not ask me why).

If the proposed construction complies with all the rules, including local design regulations, then approval will be forthcoming. This is in fact a passive action on the part of the local authority. If no refusal is issued within two months, the permission is deemed to be granted.

The building must then be started within two years. (I am convinced that this is the reason why so many building sites receive a heap of sand and then grind to a halt. The sand heap is proof of commencement and the owner can thus keep his permission going until he is ready to start the real construction work).

A copy of the planning permission is posted at the *mairie* and the number of the permit must be displayed on the site. Third parties have four months in which to lodge objections.

C. *Plan d'Occupation des Sols (P.O.S.)*

More and more properties that people buy in France fall within a zoning plan, called P.O.S. for short. These plans set out the basic planning zones within the jurisdiction of certain local authorities. In most sleepy villages in the heart of the French countryside, there is no need for such sophisticated precautions. Each planning application is considered on its merits, provided it complies with certain basic rules called *Règlement Nationale d'Urbanisme (R.N.U.)*.

However there are many localities where pressure is building up and too much building will spoil the environment. Rather than having to submit a large number of applications to an overworked planning committee, a local authority can set out in advance what can be built where and how densely. It is an efficient solution to a problem encountered by many small towns and village that attract too much attention from developers and individual house builders. The area could be a beauty spot, or one of special historic or architectural interest. These sensitive areas can be despoiled by intensive building, whose owners do not realise they are helping to destroy the very beauty they are attempting to exploit.

In fact, some quite ordinary locations have a P.O.S., since these zoning plans do not only make life easier for local planning authorities but they also allow landowners to know where they stand. The plan sets out in advance those sites that are non-constructible and others that have approval for low or high density building. It cuts out the arguments and lengthy appeals. It is a very French solution to a knotty problem.

5. RENOVATIONS AND IMPROVEMENTS

Of all the foreigners buying property in the French countryside, most will want to undertake improvements of some kind. The classic example, but getting rarer because of the diminshing stock, is the farmhouse or cottage that has had practically no modernisation since the nineteenth century. There would be no kitchen, bathroom or lavatory. Others will have had some work done on them in recent years but are still far from being up to modern standards.

All these properties then require some work and that means bringing in a builder. The normal approach would be to ask the local French estate agent who sold you the property to introduce you to the appropriate tradesmen *(artisans)* - usually a *maçon* for walls, roof and stonework, a *plombier* for plumbing and sanitary arrangements, a *menuisier* for carpentry and an *électricien* for electric wiring. For small country renovations it is necessary to hire each trade separately, although some of them double up, especially plumbers and electricians. This is possibly time-consuming. The only real problem is to get them to turn up in the right order!

The agent will arrange a meeting on site so that you can inform them of your intentions. They will then send you an estimate *(devis)*. If you accept it you will be asked to sign it and pay a deposit. It is vital that you agree a completion date and that the builder understands you intend to keep him to it.

Because of the language problem, you may be tempted to use a local British builder who has set himself up to provide renovation work for English-speaking buyers. There are quite a few of these and most are professional and fully qualified. In France builders must be registered and covered by insurance. This is important, since this provides protection against defects in the fabric of the building for a period of ten years, and in the finishings (mainly plumbing and wiring) for two years. These policies are underwritten by insurance companies, so that the protection continues, even if the builder has ceased work or gone away. A chap you meet in a bar who is working on the quiet will surely not be registered and his work not guaranteed in this way. Remember, if ever you need to resell the property, your prospective purchaser may want to establish that the improvements are still covered.

Some buyers like to do the work themselves or bring builders out from Britain.In this case make sure that the finished work is in keeping with the local style of architecture. The renovation job might satisfy you at the time, but an eventual purchaser could be more touchy about the proper use of local materials and baulk at insensitive restoration.

One of the golden rules of property is to assume that *you may one day have to sell*. Do not do anything that might make it difficult for you to achieve this and above all *do not overspend*. Always get written quotations *(devis)* beforehand and receipted invoices afterwards. You will need the latter to offset against capital gains tax in the event of a resale.

What then do these old country properties require in the way of restoration? First of all, please remember that the old farmhouse or farm cottage has been the home to a succession of hard-working farming families who have lived their entire lives in the property. It will have seen marriages and births, and been a witness to family dramas and feuds, peels of laughter will have rung out and tears shed. The homestead will have a soul. If it is in its original pre-war condition it will probably look the same as it did when originally built some two hundred years ago. The French agricultural economy has changed more since the war than in the whole preceding five hundred years.

Of course, you are the new owner and you will want to modify it to make it comfortable for you and your family. Here then are the main tasks you will have to undertake.

I am assuming that the basic structure is sound and that the shell of the property does not require rebuilding or shoring up. Even so, the roof is the first vulnerable area. Even well maintained country properties have roof problems and one that has been neglected is bound to leak at one point. This is not a problem. France gets its fair share of violent storms. These play havoc with roofs and as a consequence roof repairs and maintenance are quickly attended to by the local roof tiler *(couvreur)*. You will find him more easily in the area of France that uses Roman tiles (the russet coloured "up and over" ones to be found in a wide arc from the Charente in the west, through the south west to Provence in the south east). These tiles are not nailed to the roof timbers but simply rest one on top of the other thanks to the shallow roof pitch.

Flat tiles that are nailed to a steeper roof are less vulnerable. Those are found in the eastern Dordogne and Lot, as well as in Brittany and Normandy where slate tiles are used.

Having assured yourself that the roof is sound, you will then wish to install a modern kitchen and bathroom. You can spend as much or as little as you want here, but whatever your aspirations you will be constrained by the most down-to-earth of considerations - the septic tank. This is the universal form of drainage in the French countryside and any mistakes made at this stage could cause unpleasant and embarrassing problems later. They could even jeopardise your chances of reselling the property.

Septic tank technology
Every cottage and farmhouse in the French countryside relies on a septic tank *(fosse septique)* for its sewage disposal. It is an efficient and hygienic system but there are rules that must be followed.

The tank comes as a single unit and rarely needs emptying. The sewage is broken down by the action of anaerobic bacteria in the tank. What comes out is in theory as close to water as you can get.

In the old days, some twenty years ago, the installation was quite primitive. People took fewer baths, or it was assumed they did, showers were unheard of, and washing machines and dishwashers almost non-existent.

Not only is more expected of the system now, but manufacturers have risen to the challenge and can offer some quite sophisticated equipment.

The illustration shows the *minimum* that you must install, and at the lowest cost. Spending more on a higher quality installation may prove to be money well spent. This can be especially true if for example your plumber has assumed that you will always be occupying the property as a family of four. What would happen if a lot of friends descended on you during the summer holidays or if your tenants crammed the place with teenagers in sleeping bags.

Yes, you guessed it. A septic tank with insufficient capacity will overflow. Well, that's one way to get rid of the teenagers.

LAYOUT OF BASIC SEPTIC TANK

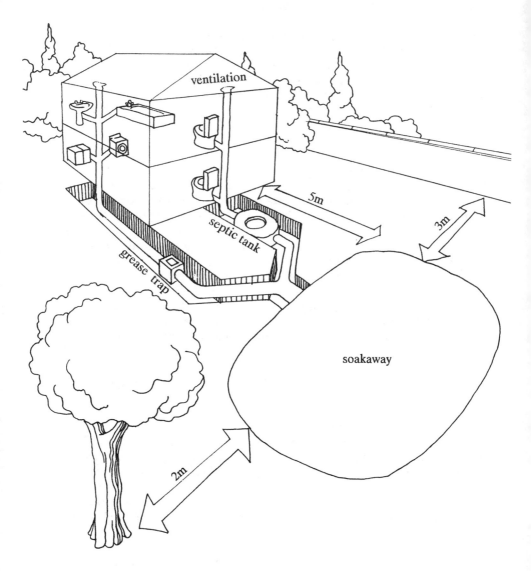

Remember also to take into account any future expansion of the property. As a general rule, the tank should measure 2 cubic metres for two bedrooms and 0.5 cubic metre for each additional bedroom.

This is how the system works. There are two sources of effluent; the soiled water from the bathroom and kitchen *(eaux usées)* and the sewage from the WC *(eaux de vannes)*. The illustration shows that the soiled water by-passes the septic tank and goes straight to the soak-away. This arrangement is becoming out of favour now and the latest version of tank can cope with all the effluent. Either way it is essential that the soiled water passes through a grease trap, especially since the advent of washing machines and the greater use of detergents. Your plumber will have to empty this regularly.

Once broken down in the septic tank, the effluent is dispersed in the soak-away. The primitive version of this would be a large hole filled with rocks and then covered over with top soil. However, there are systems now that consist of perforated tubes that discharge the waters more scientifically and safely. This is important if your soil is heavy with clay and impermeable.

There are certain rules to be observed with regard to the soak-away. It must be at least 5 metres from the house (the septic tank itself must be as close as possible). The boundary of the plot has to be more than 3 metres away.

The slope of your land is important too. A gentle slope is ideal. No slope at all and you have to dig deeper for the soak-away. If you have too steep a slope, the waters will rush away instead of dispersing gently. Your plumber will advise you.

Whichever system you select you will need to file an application with the planning office. Your plumber might laugh at this and say that in your particular locality it is not necessary. Be sure to insist that it is done. He will do it for you and it is not a complicated matter.

More often than not, the installation of a septic tank presupposes a new bathroom to go with it. Whilst new conversions (new bathrooms, kitchens, etc) do not require planning permission, it is necessary to file a declaration with the *mairie* for rating purposes. The form is H1 or H2 depending on whether it is an internal conversion or a new extension. Nine British purchasers out of ten do not know about this formality, but it should be complied with.

Renovation Grants and Improvement Subsidies

This is of the those subjects that raises hopes and then dashes them. Examples abound of grants and subsidies being handed out, but one rarely meets anyone who has actually received one. True, most official help is aimed at French residents and in most cases you need to be a French taxpayer to benefit.

Let us look first at the different forms in which these grants and subsidies come. The grants themselves are direct contributions of money that do not have to be reimbursed. Then there are soft loans which can carry an interest rate of as little as 1%. Finally, there are tax deductions allowed to those improving their properties including the installation of energy saving, and also to landlords adding to the renting stock.

Let us look at these in turn. First the **grants** *(primes)* and **subsidies** *(subventions)* which are straight monetary contributions from specialist banks and organisations whose task it is to encourage upgrading of the country's housing. The most important of these is the A.N.A.H. *(Agence Nationale pour l'Amélioration de l'Habitat)* working through a state bank, the Crédit Foncier de France.

The grants are earmarked for properties that are 20 years old or more and occupied by owners with low incomes. The maximum sum that can be provided in this category is 20% of the value of improvements not exceeding 70,000 Frs. Thus, 14,000 Frs is the most one could receive.

Owners of property that is to be let out as a main residence for periods of at least 10 years can also receive grants for improvements. The properties have to be at least 15 years old, and the amounts offered can vary from 25% to 70% of the cost. It is important not to commence work until the application has been granted by the A.N.A.H.

There are two further sources of grants that are more likely to interest foreign owners. These relate to *gîtes* and *monuments historiques*. *Gites*, as you must have surmised by now, are owner-managed holiday units in the French countryside. Some local authorities are keen to promote tourism in their locality and will provide financial assistance for the improvement of derelict accommodation or the conversion of an outbuilding such as a barn. However, this is entirely a regional policy and it is very difficult to know in advance if a certain property will qualify. You will have to knock on many doors before you get an answer and you have to be the owner of the property in question before even asking. Put out of your mind any idea of obtaining this information before deciding to buy.

You do not have to own a castle in order to qualify for subsidies paid towards *monuments historiques*. This is because the classification applies not only to the historical building itself, but also to a radius all around it. In some cases, complete villages are listed as being within the zone of a *monument historique* and all the properties there qualify. Thus if your house is within, say, 100 metres of an old chateau or church, you could get a financial contribution to repair the roof for example, or replace the windows. The object is to ensure that France's historical sites are well maintained in a suitable manner. The organisation, or person, to which applications should be directed is the *Architecte des Batiments de France* for the departement. A word of warning, however. Often the budget available for these grants is exhausted before the year is out. You are then asked to re-apply in the following year. In the meantime if your roof is leaking you have to decide whether to continue with buckets under the roof or forego the grant and get the work down. Whatever happens, you cannot apply *after* the work is started.

The second category of special assistance comes in the form of **soft loans.** Generally speaking, only taxpayers in France qualify. First are the 1 to 4% p.a. loans for improvements and extensions to one's main residence. You need to be employed in France to apply.

Many French residents pay towards a saving plan called *épargne-logement*. This qualifies you for a low cost loan at the end of the savings term. Those on low income can benefit from a *P.A.P.* loan, the purpose of which is to facilitate home ownership.

Finally there are **tax deductions** for those borrowing to improve their main residence in France. Tax payers get a tax reduction of 25% of the interest payable per annum. The maximum period is 5 years with a ceiling of 15,000 Frs, increased by 2,000 Frs for each dependant. Energy saving work such as thermal insulation and central heating controls gives rise to a tax reduction of 25% of the work value up to 8,000 Frs for an unmarried person and 16,000 Frs for a couple, plus the usual 2,000 Frs per dependant.

6. IMPORTING ONE'S BELONGINGS TO FRANCE

CITIZENS OF THE EUROPEAN UNION

Since the Single Market came into force, free entry into France with one's furniture and effects is now permitted **providing:**

- You are in possession of the certificate of ownership *(attestation de propriété)* signed by the notaire. This can be a problem for those wishing to travel with their furniture to France for the completion date. This is a cart before the horse situation, since the certificate will not be forthcoming until you complete, and you need to enter France to do so. All is not lost, however. If you find yourself in this position, you can ask the notaire for a certificate of intention to purchase *(attestation d'intention d'acquérir)*. The notaire should have no problem with this provided there is a date fixed for the final signature. If you should then be stopped by a customs official, this certificate should prove satisfactory.

- The furniture being imported must be compatible with the property you are buying. For example, if you have bought a two bedroom cottage, you cannot import furniture that is obviously destined for a six bedroom mansion. This rule is designed to prevent importation for other than the furnishing of the importer's own residence.

- The furniture must be used. If any items look new, then be sure to have receipts to show that they are at least three months old.

CITIZENS OUTSIDE THE EUROPEAN UNION

Your property in France is a secondary residence (holiday home)
It is permitted to import into France one's furniture and effects duty free. This can be done in one or more removals. In the latter case, the dates of each trip must be specified on the original application. The following procedure must be observed:

1. An application form can be obtained from the French Consulate. It has to be forwarded to the regional customs office (*Direction régionale des Douanes*) of the area in which the property is situated. The addresses of these regional offices are provided with the form.

The importer will need to provide the following information on the form:
(a) Home address (outside France).
(b) Address of the property in France with a statement indicating whether it is leased or owned (if it is leased, then it must be for a period of at least twelve months).
(c) The condition and age of the furniture and effects. New items must be listed and are not included in the duty free allowance.
(d) Port of entry in which customs clearance will take place.

The application form has to be accompanied by an inventory in French in triplicate with the value of each item indicated in French francs. The total value must also be provided. The inventory has to carry the following declaration (in French): "I, the undersigned, hereby declare that the above mentioned items have been my property for more than three months, that they are for my personal use in my secondary residence and that they come from my own residence in [your country of residence]".

All new items and anything on the following list do not qualify for the duty-free concession. They must be listed separately and will be subject to payment of *TVA* (French Value Added Tax) on importation.

> Tobacco and tobacco products
> Alcoholic beverages and products
> Food stocks
> Hi-fi equipment
> Motor vehicles
> Airplanes, boats and mobile homes (trailers)
> Fitted kitchens, building materials and garden tools
> (your outdoor barbecue might be disqualified too).

You must also supply evidence that your principal residence is in your home country. If you pay local property taxes, a copy of the demand should suffice.

The application form should also be accompanied by a certificate of ownership from the notaire. This can be a Catch 22 problem for those who want to complete their purchase and take possession with their furniture at the same time. The certificate cannot be issued by the notaire until completion and the furniture cannot be imported until the certificate is issued. (However, see above on how to obtain a certificate of intention to purchase).

2. Once the regional customs office has replied to the application with an approval, the following documents must be presented for customs clearance at the port of entry:
(a) the inventory in French that will have been returned to you stamped and approved.
(b) if importing non-exempt items, form Cerfa 30-1584 which they will give you on the spot.

At the port of entry, the customs may just wave the vehicle through, but if they ask to inspect the contents, it may be necessary to appoint a customs agent at the quayside, who will have to be paid a fee. There could be a delay of 2 to 4 hours. There is nothing for it then but to go to a café and enjoy the first coffee and croissants of the trip.

Your house in France will be your main residence
Non-residents of the European Union who intend to take up residence in France may apply to import their furniture and effects into France free of duty. One must first obtain a **certificate of change of residence** from the French Consulate. For this, the following conditions have to be fulfilled:
1. A photocopy of the importer's passport must be submitted (showing personal details, issue and expiry dates).
2. Evidence of residence in your home country must be supplied. This can be a declaration by an electoral registrar, or a copy of a demand for local property taxes. The applicant's nationality, home address and length of residence must be stated.
3. If you are going to France to work, you need to submit your contract of employment. If you intend to be self-employed, you need to get a *carte de séjour* which can only be obtained in France.
4. If you do not intend to work in France, then you have to submit a *visa d'établissement* for which prior application must be made to the French Consulate.
5. A separate declaration that the imported items will not be sold has to appear on a form that is supplied by the French Consulate.

Once you have received your *attestation de changement de résidence*, you can proceed to draw up an inventory of the items you wish to take over with you. You will need two copies of the inventory in French with the value of each item shown in French francs and a figure for the total value. The inventories have to carry a declaration that all the items have been in the applicant's possession for at least three months (six months in the case of private motor cars, mobile homes, pleasure craft and private airplanes), and that they are for the importer's own use and will not be sold or otherwise disposed of for at least twelve months from the date of importation. The declaration has to appear in French thus: *Je déclare que ces objets et biens de valeur en cours d'usage m'appartiennent depuis plus de trois mois (six mois pour ma voiture) et sont bien destinés à mon utilisation personnelle.* This document must be signed and dated.

Garden tools and outdoor equipment (including the barbecue) do not qualify for tax-free importation, but they should still be featured on the inventory.

You will need the following papers when you go through French Customs:
1. *Attestation de changement de résidence* issued by the French Consulate.
2. The two copies of the inventory.
3. If you are importing valuables or a motor vehicle, you will need to complete form Cerfa 30-1584 on the spot. Proof of ownership and the registration document of the car will also have to be provided as well as evidence that it is fully duty paid in your home country.

The Customs will then return to you one copy of the inventory duly stamped (hang on to it). If you are importing your car, they will also give you clearance certificate 846A to enable you to register it at the Prefecture of your new residence.

You want to bring your car, motor cycle or caravan with you
Only those taking up permanent residence in France can bring their cars into France duty- free. However, since cars in France are relatively cheap and since you may end up with a car that has little resale value in France (certainly a British right hand drive car will be almost unsellable), most people now feel it more cost effective to sell their car back home before leaving and then buy a French registered one on arrival in France. However, those who do wish to bring their cars into France on changing residence must comply with the following rules:
- the vehicle must have been registered in your name, duty paid, for at least six months. After importing it into France, the car cannot be lent, sold or alienated in any way for at least 12 months. The details of the vehicle must be listed on your inventory even if imported separately.

7. INSURANCE

It is important to remember that it is mandatory for householders in France to be covered by insurance, especially in respect of Third Party Liability. If you are buying an individual house (not a *copropriété*) be sure to check the draft conveyance document to see if provision is made for the existing policy to be cancelled or not. Usually the notaire will ask for a policy number at the time of completion. Certainly if you are taking out a mortgage, the lender will need to be satisfied that insurance cover has been taken out.

One thing to bear in mind is that French owners tend to under-insure, so my recommendation is that you specify your own arrangements. This can be done through a local French insurance agent (the estate agent can help here) or you can take out insurance in the U.K.

If you take out a policy in Britain, the advantage is that the policy will be written in English, the premiums payable in sterling, but most important of all any claims you make will be in English in England instead of in French by long distance correspondence. English policies may not be so suitable for those living in France permanently, in which case a local French insurer should fit the bill.

Many French policies cover **buildings** not on the basis of value but on the size of the property (either according to the number of rooms or to the habitable surface area in square metres). In this way the company undertakes to replace like with like in the event of fire or other damage. There is usually a built-in premium increase to allow for inflation, without reference to any rise in property values. As for **contents**, any item of high value has to be itemised. Many French owners keep photographs of their choicest pieces, which the companies welcome in the event of a claim.

Most French household policies are called *multirisques-habitation*, but be careful to check that all buildings are included. If you have a separate outbuilding, a barn or garage, say, be sure to notify the insurer. Similarly, the existence of a swimming pool should be declared, since pool risks include freezing and accidental drowning.

While on the subject of frost, I would stress the importance of not underestimating the severity of some winters in France. Although the summers may be hotter than anything you have encountered at home, the winters can be much colder too. Even in the deep south, a sharp frost can freeze your water pipes or worse still the water meter itself. If the latter bursts in your absence, you could end up with a serious leak and run up a high bill before the damage is discovered and reported to you. Remember, in France you have to pay for mains water according to consumption.

Owners of flats in a *copropriété* will find that basic buildings cover will be included as part of the common services and the premium included in the service charges. Details of this will be supplied in the *réglement de copropriété*. The flat owner will of course have to make his own arrangements with regard to insurance of contents. Occasionally, an apartment comes on the market as part of a subdivision of a larger villa or town house. There may be only three or four units in all and care should be taken to check on what may or may not be communally insured. These small subdivisions are not subject to the same stringent condominium rules as the larger and newer developments.

You should be aware that if you wish to cancel your policy, the onus is on the insured to serve notice on the company. You cannot just let the policy lapse at the time of renewal, since the cover will automatically remain in force at the expiry of each year unless you notify the insurers formally by registered letter with advice of reception of delivery (the usual method for serving notice in France). Be careful, you must send the letter in good time with anything from 30 to 60 days advance notice, depending on the policy.

8. MORTGAGES

If it is your intention to purchase a French property with the help of mortgage finance, you will more likely than not be borrowing from a French bank. This is for the simple reason that the property to be mortgaged is in France, and a non-French bank will have difficulty in calling in its security in the event of foreclosure. Even if the bank bears an English name, it is its French subsidiary that will do the lending and consequently will have to follow the normal French procedures.

Many French banks are now represented abroad. Certainly in Great Britain they have brought out application forms in English and a generally more "user friendly" approach. (One wonders why, if they can streamline their paperwork abroad, they do not do so in France). The advantage of applying through a representative office in your home country is that all the queries can be sorted out conveniently and promptly without engaging in long distance correspondence.

If, on the other hand, you do make an application to a local bank in France (at the instigation, say, of the French agent or notaire), you may find that they treat you as if you lived locally. It is not uncommon for a local bank to ask you to call in on them in person, long after you have submitted your application and without a thought given to the fact that you live in a different country and would have to take time off work, make travel plans, etc.

The banks that provide French mortgages to non-French buyers tend to operate in accordance with the following basic rules of thumb:

- The maximum amount loaned is usually 80%
- The term is usually 5-15 years
- The amount loaned will carry with it instalments not exceeding 30% of the borrower's income before tax but after outgoings. In other words, if an applicant's income is £1,000 per month before tax and he is already paying £200 p.m. on a domestic mortgage, then only a loan with repayments of less than £240 p.m. would be contemplated.

As a rule banks prefer to lend only on a house that is in habitable condition. However, there are some banks that will lend on both the purchase and the improvements provided the total loan does not exceed 70% of the whole cost - purchase plus renovations. It is normal, naturally, when buying a house in France to borrow in French francs. The conventional arrangement is for the instalments to be constant with a fixed rate of interest. The advantage is that since the repayments never alter, despite general interest rate fluctuations, the borrower can budget more precisely. The disadvantage is that if general interest rates fall, then the borrower ends up paying over the market rate. Conversely if they rise, he makes big savings. On the other hand, some loan packages at variable interest rates are now available, as are those with tapered repayments.

The costs surrounding a French mortgage can be high. The charge (*garantie hypothécaire*) has to be incorporated in a notarised deed of mortage and registered. The notaire's fee and costs will amount to 2-4% of the amount borrowed. These legal charges have to be added to the general conveyancing costs.

When purchasing a new property off-plan with stage payments to be made as the building progresses, the mortgage is registered at the time of the original conveyance but the funds drawn upon as and when required. It is important that the lending bank is aware of this, otherwise you will be lent the full amount prematurely attracting unnecessary interest charges.

The advantage of a French mortgage of course is that you use the security of the French property itself. On the other hand, if you have plenty of equity in your property at home, it may be more cost effective to **remortgage** that. You could save considerably on legal charges although there could be an arrangement fee of some kind to pay. It would probably also be quicker to arrange. Remember, if you are remortgaging outside France, as far as the French are concerned you will be considered a cash purchaser.

If you are self-employed, you will have to submit accounts. French banks still have a problem with accountant's letters - they usually prefer something more official. Also if you are planning to live in France and earn a living there, the bank will not be happy to lend to you until your future income is established.

9. TAXATION IN FRANCE

I would like to state from the outset that the matter of taxation is necessarily complicated and that a résumé such as is given below cannot hope to cover all the aspects of every person's financial position. However, there are four basic categories of tax that affect a purchaser of French property:

- Non-residents of France buying a holiday home *(résidence secondaire)*
- Those taking up retirement in France
- Working residents in France (salary earners and self-employed)
- Business taxes (including *gites* and B&B)
- Other taxes (wealth, capital gains, inheritance & local)

Generally it can be said that taxation of income is low in France, although the French themselves find this hard to believe. On the other hand, VAT *(TVA)* is high at 18.6% with very few exceptions.

1. THOSE BUYING A HOLIDAY HOME
Since it is one's main residence that determines where one pays one's income tax, persons in this category will have little to concern them here, with the possible exception of those letting out their properties when not in occupation, including leaseback owners.

Holiday Rentals. These will fall into two categories:
Most purchasers of **individual rural properties** will let to British or other North European tenants either by advertising direct or through a travel company. French holiday-makers are not interested in renting these houses and if they were they would not pay the same high rents. The demand for French country holidays, particularly from the British, is well established.

Now the rules state that it is the location of the property that determines the tax jurisdiction and this means that holiday rentals in France are a matter for the French taxman. However, as often happens, many British owners let to British tenants with an English contract and payment made in Britain. Consequently that is where the income is likely to be declared. The Anglo-French double tax agreement would then protect the owner from any demands that could be made on him in France. However, owners should watch for a change of attitude on the part of French tax officials, since the matter of income from French property remaining untaxed France is exercising their minds. I think they will tighten up on the current loose arrangements.

Purchasers of **modern resort property**, especially in new developments, will probably have the local managing and/or letting agent handle the rentals. This is because there is a wider demand, both international and domestic, for coastal and winter sports holidays. The local agent can take care of the management and all the details. He will charge for his trouble, taking both a commission for arranging the tenancy and a management fee for the rest. Once a month or once a quarter the owner is provided with a nett remittance. The agent will deduct at source tax at 25% on this income and of course in this case the double taxation agreement comes into play again to allow the owner to escape tax at home on that particular slice of income.

Leaseback owners of modern property fall within a special tax category. They have to account once a year for the rent they have received, either in cash or in kind. This involves the tedious business of filing a tax return once a year, but the better organised French developers offer a special service which takes all the paperwork off the clients' hands. Rutherfords, the French agents, also provide an administration service for leaseback owners as well as for all those requiring help when dealing with the local bureaucracy, all for a reasonable annual fee.

2. THOSE TAKING UP RETIREMENT

The income in this category will naturally consist of pensions, life annuities and dividends from shares and securities. I would not for a minute put myself forward as being qualified to advise anyone in the matter of investments. This is work for a specialist and anyone contemplating retirement in France should seek the advice of their financial adviser as to the optimum deployment of their capital for tax mitigation. I shall confine myself to outlining the basics.

Your UK state pension will be paid to you in France from Britain without any tax being deducted (unless it is in respect of government service). It will be taxed in France, however, at the rates shown in section 3 below. You will benefit from the same 10% + 20% allowances also described below.

Your income from private investments will be taxed in France in the same way. However, since most dividends from British securities are taxed at source in UK, it is important to get advice on how to invest in stocks, including UK government stocks, where tax is not witheld at source. Any income that is surplus to the maintenance of your lifestyle in France should be confined to tax havens including the Channel Islands.

3. WORKING RESIDENTS (SALARIED PERSONS & SELF-EMPLOYED)

By attempting to guide you through the French taxation maze, I am making myself a hostage to fortune. By the time you read this, the rules may have changed and the rates altered. However, by setting out the ground rules for 1995, I hope to be able to give you an indication of how the system works and how much it is likely to cost you.

The calculation of net taxable income is in many ways fairer than in many other countries. For example, social security contributions are tax deductible (unlike National Insurance contributions in Britain).

In addition, there is an allowance *(déduction forfaitaire)* of 10% of revenue for "professional expenses" with a minimum allowance of 2,190 Frs and a maximum permitted of 73,270 Frs. An additional allowance *(abbatement général)* of 20% is deductible over and above the first 10% on taxable income up to 667,000 Frs. If you are employed by a company in which you have more than 35% of the shares, this second allowance may be reduced to 10%.

Tax rates. The rates given below are for single persons with no dependants. The rates are then subject to various coefficients in the case of taxpayers who are married and/or have dependants. A single taxpayer has a coefficient of 1. His or her spouse brings it up to 2. Each of the first two dependent children is worth a ½ point and thereafter each child is worth 1 point. Thus a married couple with two dependent children have a coefficient of 3, but with three children it becomes 4. A widowed or divorced taxpayer with one child has 2 and with two children it becomes 2½.

To calculate the tax due, divide your taxable income by the coefficient, then work out the tax before multiplying back the resultant figure by the coefficient (no, you do not end up with the figure you started with, the higher the coefficient, the bigger the reduction).

INCOME TAX PAYABLE ON A COEFFICIENT OF 1

Tranche of nett income after allowances

From	To	Rate %
0	22,210F	0.00
48,570	85,480F	25.00
85,480	138,410F	35.00
138,410	225,210F	45.00
225,210	277,730F	50.00
over	277,730F	56.80

Further allowances are applicable for mortgage interest, life assurance, childminding expenses, etc.

Finally, there are further allowances in favour of the low paid, and each profession has its own special treatment with other allowances. And remember to divide by your coefficient. You will observe that although the tax percentage rates are relatively high, the nett amounts of tax payable are quite low.

4. BUSINESS TAXES
In France, the treatment of businesses for administrative and tax purposes is not as flexible or uniform as in Britain. Each type of activity tends to be pigeonholed by category and its taxation applied differently. Putting yourself into the wrong pigeon hole will almost certainly result in the loss of tax allowances at best or even tax penalties at worst.

Generally speaking, however, the self-employed are taxed in one of the following three ways:

1. Very small businesses *(micro-entreprises)*
If your turnover does not exceed 70,000 F (net of TVA) the taxable profit is reduced automatically by 50%, with a minimum reduction of 2,000 F. Most small businesses, however, prefer to opt for the next category.

2. Flat rate tax *(forfait)*

This category is limited to those earning no more than 150,000 F *(inclusive* of TVA). In this event, accounts do not have to be submitted in the usual way. The tax assessment is a flat rate levy based on what that business would normally earn net. For both small firms and tax gatherers, this represents a saving in administration costs.

3. Simplified accounts *(bénéfice réel simplifié)*

This is a half way house between the flat rate assessment and the full scale submission of profit and loss accounts. Businesses that can be assessed in this fashion are those that do not qualify for the flat rate tax and those whose earnings are between 150,000 F and 1,100,000 F (there are some exceptions). Only very simple accounts need be kept (basically a cash book recording receipts and outgoings). Each item of expenditure, however, must be supported by an invoice or receipt.

4. Full accounts *(bénéfice réel normal)*

Businesses that qualify are those with earnings in excess of 1,100,000 F and those not wishing to opt for the simplified procedure described in (3) above.

The following types of businesses fall within the category of self-employed.

Artisans, or craftsmen *(artisans)*. Self-employed builders, plumbers and electricians are included here.

Trading activities *(activités commerciales)*. Included here are shop-keeping activities that involve the buying and selling of goods, agents and brokers, camp site owners and persons buying and selling property for gain *(marchands de biens)*.

Professional persons have their own classification. In France self-employed professionals such as accountants, lawyers and architects are classified as *professions libérales* and are treated each in a separate way.

5. WEALTH TAX

This tax called *Impôt de Solidarité sur la Fortune (ISF)* applies only to those assets situated in France. Non-French owners who are resident outside France are therefore unlikely to be affected.

The taxable threshold is 4,530,000 F and anyone contemplating the purchase of an expensive property that might bring them within the scope of the tax should consider putting it, or part of it, in the names of their children, provided there are more than one and are not dependent. The spouse is not considered as a separate part owner for the purposes of this tax (nor is a common-law spouse for that matter).

If, for any reason, you do find yourself assessed, there are certain allowances to take into account:

a) The tax payable is reduced by 1,000 F for each dependant.

b) The taxable worth does not include "professional assets" (*biens professionnels*). These can include shares in a company in which the taxpayer plays an active part and provided they amount to at least 25% of the equity. Companies having property investment as their principal activity, however, are excluded.

c) Antiques over 100 years old are exempt, as are art collections (one or more paintings for example).

d) The wealth tax, when added to the amount of income tax, cannot exceed 85% of the taxpayer's income.

The rates of walth tax are as follows:

Up to 4,530,000 F	0 %
4,530,000 F to 7,370,000 F	0.5%
7,370,000 F to 14,620,000 F	0.7%
14,620,000 F to 22,690,000 F	0.9%
22,690,000 F to 43,940,000 F	1.2%
Over 43,940,000 F	1.5%

The incidence of this tax is therefore not too onerous. For example, if your property is worth 6 million F, you pay only on the tranche above 4½ million F (joint ownership with your spouse counts as one owner). The tax due on the 1½ million F is 7,350 F and if you have two dependent children this would be reduced by a further 2,000 F.

6. DEATH DUTIES

The whole subject of inheritance and wills is the subject of another chapter in this book. This section deals purely with the tax rates.

Any *inter-vivos* gifts before the decease are accumulated and have to be entered on the estate duty return.

Non-residents of France only have to pay duty on their real property situated in France. Their movable assets the country are exempt. Residents of France, on the other hand, are assessed on all their estate.

Legacies received by *each* son or daughter are taxed as follows:

- the first 300,000 F received by each beneficiary is exempt.
- thereafter the next 50,000 F is taxed at   5%
- from 50,000 F to 75,000 F the rate is   10%
- from 75,000 F to 100,000 F the rate is   15%
- from 100,000 F to 3,400,000 F   20%
- from 3,400,000 F to 5,600,000 F   30%
- from 5,600,000 F to 11,200,000 F   35%
- over 11,200,000 F   40%

Legacies received by the spouse are taxed as follows:

- the first 330,000 F is exempt
- thereafter the next 50,000 F is taxed at   5%
- from 50,000 F and 100,000 F the rate is   10%
- from 100,000 F to 200,000 F the rate is   15%
- from 200,000 F to 3,400,000 F   20%
- from 3,400,000 F and 5,600,000 F   30%
- from 5,600,000 F and 11,200,000 F   35%
- over 11,200,000 F   40%

Between brothers and sisters the rate is 35% up to 150,000 F, and 45% thereafter, with an exemption for the first 100,000 F.

Between uncles, aunts, nephews, nieces, great uncles, great aunts, great nephews, great nieces and first cousins the rate is 55%, with an exemption for the first 10,000 F.

Between distant relatives and persons not related to the deceased it is 60%, with an exemption for the first 10,000 F. Unmarried couples should beware since they fall into this category. Payment in death duties of 60% of the deceased's half share could force the survivor to sell the property. A useful way to safeguard against this eventuality is to take out life assurance for each party in favour of the other.

Further modest allowances are granted to beneficiaries who have three or more children.

Disabled persons have an allowance of 300,000 F irrespective of the blood relationship with the deceased.

Exemptions include (i) the beneficiaries of life assurance contracted by the deceased, (ii) new residential buildings that have not hitherto been transferred (e.g. if bought off-plan by the deceased), (iii) legacies to government bodies and charitable institutions, and (iv) where the deceased was a victim of terrorism or AIDS.

Woods and forests are valued at 25% of their market value.

The Anglo-French Double Taxation Agreement is applicable so that there is no danger of double assessment.

6. LOCAL TAXES

Residential Property Taxes

Rates (property taxes) in France are levied in two ways:

Taxe Foncière or *Impôt Foncier* is the freeholder's, or owner's, tax. This is paid by whoever appears on the Land Registry title document. When you buy your property, your name and address will automatically be passed on to the local rating office. Be sure to notify them of any subsequent change of address. When a house is sold, the current year's tax is usually apportioned *pro rata* between the previous and new owners.

Newly built properties are exempt of this tax for the first two years, although a small amount for refuse (garbage) collection may still be levied. Not many people know that this exemption also applies to extensions and barn conversions, provided the owner completes and returns forms H1 or H2.

Taxe d'Habitation is payable by the occupier, either the owner himself as owner-occupier or tenant (but not holiday tenants) provided there is a properly drawn up lease or tenancy agreement *(bail d'habitation)*. In the event of a sale, there is no apportionment, since whoever is in residence on 1st January pays for the whole year.

Business Property Tax

This is called *Taxe Professionnelle* and is levied on all business premises in place of the *Taxe d'Habitation*. Since most offices and shops are rented, this would be the only property tax due by a business, the *Taxe Foncière* being paid by the landlord. However, some residential owners find themselves having to pay *Taxe Professionnelle* and this can come as a nasty surprise. This is how it comes about.

In the last few years it has become advantageous to buy modern resort property on a "leaseback" basis. Having bought your apartment or villa by the sea or in the mountains, you lease it back to the developer who then rents it out. The benefit to the buyer is that the Value Added Tax *(T.V.A.)* within the purchase price is refunded to him, or even deducted from the purchase price in the form of a discount. It is a good way of buying an asset at less than its true cost, the discount being 15% or in some cases 30%. However, the lease is a formal tenancy contract that gives the owner the status of professional landlord and that makes him liable to *Taxe Professionnelle*. In mitigation, however, he does not have to pay any *Taxe d'Habitation*.

7. CAPITAL GAINS TAX ON THE SALE OF PROPERTY

First the exemptions:
1. No capital gains tax is due on the sale of a **principal residence** in France that has been occupied by the owner for at last 5 years, or since its purchase or if he is forced to sell for family reasons.
2. **Secondary residences** too in cases where the owner does not own his principal residence (ie. if he is a tenant or if he owns a leasehold property as his main residence).
3. Property that has been owned for 22 years or more.

Resales within two years of original purchase
In these cases, the capital gain is treated as income and taxed accordingly. However, deductible expenses include the legal charges, agency commission and cost of improvements.

Resales within 2 and 22 years
The same deductible expenses are allowed as above. With regard to cost of improvements, it will be necessary to supply receipted invoices issued by the builders. These have to be official with the appropriate rate of V.A.T. *(TVA)* shown. The "back of an envelope" type of receipt will not be accepted by the tax office, nor will estimates *(devis)*, unless

these have been officially receipted. So remember to hang on to these valuable bits of paper. Many an owner has rued his lack of foresight after a frantic search for receipts that could have saved him thousands in tax.

Many people like to do some "doing up" themselves. Can this input be made tax deductible? The answer is yes, provided there are receipts for materials (eg. paint, timber, etc). The value of these materials is then multiplied by 3.

In addition there are some generous allowances:

1. The capital gains tax is reduced by 5% for each year of ownership beyond the second year. Thus after 12 years of ownership the gain is reduced by half and after 22 years it disappears altogether.

2. In addition there is a standard flat rate allowance of 6,000 F.

3. In the case of secondary residences, any interest paid on a loan is deductible for the first ten years, with a top limit of 9,000 F plus 1,500 F for each dependent child.

4. If the secondary residence is the first one owned in France and it has been in his possession for at least five years, and if the taxpayer rents and does not own his main residence at home, then there are further allowances amounting to to 20,000 F for the owner plus another 20,000 F for his spouse and 10,000 F for each living child. (Single, divorced or widowed owners are entitled to 30,000 F). This allowance can rarely be claimed, of course, since most people own their main homes. However, in Britain, some own a lease on a flat and as leaseholders they qualify as non-owners and can claim this allowance.

How the capital gains tax is paid

Non-resident taxpayers have to pay the capital gains tax out of the proceeds of the house sale, and this is witheld by the notaire. The computation of the tax is made by him, but the local tax office reserves the right to claim additional tax in the event of a miscalulation in the assessment. Since the non-resident taxpayer will have by then sold up and disappeared, he has to appoint a representative in France who will stand as guarantor. Few of us are blessed with friends who are both resident in France and substantial enough (as well as trusting!) to sign an open-ended guarantee, and this can be a problem.

Fortunately, however, if the transaction is a simple one and it is plain that no complications are likely to arise after the notaire's initial computation, the local tax office will grant a dispensation (*dispense*) of the need to appoint a guarantor. If the exemption is not forthcoming and no other solution can be found, it is possible to appoint a professional guarantor for a fee.

10. HEALTH, MEDICAL AND SOCIAL SECURITY

Health Care

I will divide into 7 categories those who will require health care while in France:-

- Tourists
- Those employed by a French employer
- Those working in France for a short period while remaining employed by a European Union employer
- Those going to live, but not work, in France in advance of retirement (under the age of 65 years)
- Retired persons (over 65 years)
- Self-employed

Tourists who are nationals of a EU country are covered by the E111 form (obtainable in UK from the post office). Those whose visits to France do not exceed 182 days (6 months) in any one year, nor for three months at a time, are deemed to be tourists. Until such time then that you obtain your *carte de séjour*, you will fall into this category.

Those **employed by a French employer** have to make contributions that are deducted from the pay packet. The employer will also have to make substantial contributions on your behalf. As an employee in France your registration with the Social Security will be routine.

Those working in France for a short period while **remaining employed by a EU employer.** Employees in this category can escape having to register in France and continue to pay contributions at home. Your employer should supply you with form E101 to prove that you are making your contributions. You can then obtain treatment in France under form E111 (as for tourists). There is a time limit for those in this category.

Those in **pre-retirement** need to obtain form E106 from Newcastle. This will give you cover in France for a limited time depending on your contributions in your home country. Thereafter you will have to subscribe to private insurance until such time as you reach the age of 65.

Retired persons who have made all their contributions at home can register with the Social Security and receive health care on the same basis as French pensioners. You will have to produce form E121 to prove your entitlement.

Self-employed persons in France must make special contributions and rely heavily on private insurance in order to be fully covered. People in this category get a raw deal in my view, but the French civil service assumes that the self-employed do not declare all their ill-gotten gains and that it all evens out in the end.

Note: *References to E forms apply to nationals of EU countries only.*
       In Britain the DSS Overseas Branch is at Longbenton, Newcastle
       upon Tyne, NE98 1YX
       (Tel. 0191 225 3827).

Whichever of the above categories you fall into, you will have to follow the same procedure when claiming for health care on French social security.

Unlike the British system, where you are registered with one doctor in your locality and your treatment is free (with a charge made for pre-scribed drugs), in France you pay first out of your pocket and then claim a refund. An advantage of the French system is that you can choose your doctor and because payment has to be made there and then, it cuts out the time wasters. Waiting lists are rare in France.

The problem is that the refund is only partial, from 60% to 80% (see box below). It is necessary to have top-up insurance to cover the difference.

First, let me explain how to claim for the basic Social Security refund. Later in this chapter, I will deal with top-up insurance.

Your first visit to the doctor will cost 110 F. He must be *conventionné* which means he is registered with the Social Security. You will be given a *feuille de soins* which details the treatment you have received and the amount paid. If medecine has been prescribed, you must remove the detachable label from the container (*vignette*) and stick it on the *feuille de soins*. This identifies the drug and the cost. You then

Type of treatment or consultation	Percentage refund
Practitioner's fee (doctor, dentist, etc)	70%
Auxiliary's fee (eg. nurse)	60%
Analyses & laboratory reports	60%
Rare medicines	100%
Routine medicines	65%
Out-patient hospital consultation	70%
X-ray	70%
Hospitalisation (up to 30 days)	80%
Hospitalisation (beyond 30 days)	100%
Hospital surgery	100%

send the form to the local C.P.A.M. (*Caisse Primaire d'Assurance Maladie*). If you are a tourist you also send in your form E111. If you are registered, then your social security number will be on the *feuille de soins*. In a month or so you should get your refund.

If you are treated as a patient in a hospital, you will not have to fork out the full cost, which of course could be quite substantial. The percentage covered by the Social Security will not be charged and you will pay only for the balance (*ticket modérateur*). This is where your **top-up insurance** comes in.

Most French people make their top-up insurance arrangements with one of the long established provident funds, called *Mutuelles*. Being non-profit making, these funds have to reflect the true costs of treatment in each locality as well as the incidence of claims. Thus in a region with a lot of elderly people the fund's outgoings could be higher and the premiums charged would reflect that. There are many of these *mutuelles* and one can shop around.

Some British people prefer to insure the top-up with a more familiar insurance company, such as Norwich Union Healthcare, that offers a special scheme for European countries. The cost would be greater than a *mutuelle* but the cover wider ranging. As a guide, a *mutuelle* would charge someone over 40 years an annual premium of £300+ whereas an insurance company would require £400-£600.

Whatever happens, if you are British and have left the UK, you cannot go back for free treatment (although you will be treated free for emergencies sustained while in the country).

PENSIONS

When you retire, you will be receiving both a state retirement pension and probably also an occupational pension linked to your previous employment.

State retirement pension

If you are entitled to a UK retirement pension or widow's benefit, you can draw it in France at the same rate as would be paid at home. You must produce form E121 to prove your entitlement. If you move to France before you have completed the full contributions record of 44 out of the 49 years of your working life (39 out of 44 if you are a woman), you can continue to pay contributions voluntarily in order to maintain your right to a full British state pension.

You will not pay tax in UK on your state pension, unless you were in government employment.
You will, however, have to pay tax in France but only on 70% or thereabouts of the amount received. For the rate of tax payable, see the chapter in this book on taxation.

11. TAKING UP PERMANENT RESIDENCE IN FRANCE

First a word of warning. The official procedure to follow for applying to take up permanent residence in France is clearly set out. However, many applicants have reported widely different experiences. For while some have whistled through, others have come up against an obstacle course of almost Kafka-like complexity. The problem is that interpretation of the rules can differ from region to region and even between officials within the same department. My advice therefore is not to rely too much on one person's experience, but to proceed in accordance with the rules. A measure of optimism and perseverance will help.

CITIZENS OF THE EUROPEAN UNION

Retirement
There was a time when it was best to make prior application to the Visa Section of the French Consulate before setting off for France to take up permanent residence. Now, however, it is generally considered much more practical to sort everything out once one has settled in at one's new home. The reason is that the local procedures are much more simplified and that it is easier to deal direct with the appropriate office.

Having moved into your new house, you need to apply for your temporary residence permit *(carte de séjour)* within two months. You should first go to the local town hall *(mairie)*. If it is too small to cope with the application (as many village *mairies* are) then you will be directed to the *préfecture*. As usual you will need the appropriate documentation, namely:-
- Valid passport,
- Birth certificate,
- Marriage certificate (if appropriate),
- 3 passport photographs (it is always a good idea to have a plentiful supply of these),
- Proof of accommodation in France,
- Proof of current residence. Remember, in this interim period you

are not yet officially a resident of France and your home must be elsewhere. Even if you have sold your house at home, you are deemed by the French still to have a residence outside France. It is best therefore to bring with you your latest Council Tax (home property tax) demand which will serve as proof of your residence outside France.
- Proof of existence. This is a real puzzler for Anglo-Saxons and highlights a crucial difference between our attitudes and those of Continental Europe. One of my clients suggested to the nice lady at the counter that she should pinch him. If he felt any pain and yelped, then yes, he did exist. Not good enough. A complete *dossier* requires proof that you do indeed exist and for that you must supply your birth certificate. In Britain it is easy to adopt a false identity. Not so in France.
- Finally you have to provide proof of income.

Having obtained your *carte de séjour* it will be valid for one year and must be renewed. Be sure to apply for renewal two months before expiry of the current permit. After you have lived in France with a *carte de séjour* for three years, you apply for a *carte de résident*. This will be valid for ten years and is renewable. Application for a *carte de résident* should be made three months before expiry of the *carte de séjour*.

Wage earners
Citizens of the European Union have no restrictions on seeking employment in France, provided application is made for a *carte de séjour*.

The procedure is the same as above, but instead of a bank statement showing proof of income, you have to supply a contract of employment, assuming you have a job already or one lined up.

Self-employed persons
Again, citizens of the European Union are free to set up in business or carry out self-employed activity in France (see chapter 13 on Business in France). One must remember, however, that many activities are regulated, or if not, require registration with an appropriate professional or trade body. In many cases, it is enough to register with the *Chambre des Métiers*, eg. for those in the building trade, or the *Chambre de Commerce*. In any event the chambers of commerce in France are very helpful and a visit to the local chamber is a must for anyone contemplating a business venture. Otherwise, to obtain a *carte de séjour* you need to follow the same procedure set out above.

CITIZENS OUTSIDE THE EUROPEAN UNION

Since differing rules apply in different countries, I am going to be unhelpful by saying that you should apply to your local French Consulate (it may be in a distant town) and obtain from them the information that applies to persons of your nationality. The basic rules set out above will still apply to you, but there may be variations. Generally, though, I would recommend that you make all your arrangements in advance and do not leave them until you arrive in France.

12. JOINT OWNERSHIP, WILLS & INHERITANCE

Over recent years a number of myths have been put about with regard to the treatment of a French property upon the death of its owner. There are two matters that require consideration, French inheritance rules and tax. I shall endeavour in this chapter to provide definitive information and lay to rest the half truths.

First the French laws of succession. If you planned to leave your property to a chorus girl, think again. In France, your children have absolute priority over your estate, even over your surviving spouse.

Like many British purchasers, you may want to buy your property jointly with your spouse; and in the event of the decease of one party your intention could be to have that half share pass on to the survivor. The problem is that your children will have a prior claim to part of the deceased's share (the proportion depends on how many children there are). Naturally, it may be your intention to have them inherit the property eventually but in the meantime you would prefer that full title devolves to your spouse.

The situation can be complicated if there are children from a previous marriage. They too would have a claim on their deceased parent's French estate, leaving the surviving spouse to share the property with persons from whom he or she may be estranged. And if they were minors, only the French courts could authorise a disposal.

Similarly, if two or more unmarried people buy a property jointly, then their descendants and even ascendants would have to inherit, even though the intention may have been to bequeath the share to the surviving joint-owner. In France the rule is that it is illegal to disinherit your blood relatives. Or is it?

In fact, you can make prior arrangements in order to ensure that a joint owner will inherit the deceased's share. Provided the notaire is instructed to insert an accrual clause into the title *before* you purchase, your intentions can be carried out. This clause is otherwise known as a *tontine*. This is how it works.

Purchasers A and B wish to purchase a French property and own it jointly (in fact they would each own a share, say 50%, as tenants in common - *en indivis*). A and B do not have to be married to each other and they can be of the same sex. The intention is that on the demise of one or other, his or her share should pass on to the survivor, without any relatives getting involved.

Accordingly, the notaire will be instructed to insert into the conveyance document a *clause tontine*. The effect of this clause is that on the death of A or B, the survivor is deemed to be the sole owner and the first never to have been owner at all.

If you planned to leave your property to a chorus girl, think again.

It is a neat arrangement, but there are disadvantages. On the death of the second party, the property would be inherited by that person's heirs. The first deceased's children would not inherit any part of the property. Also if A and B have children from the current marriage but B also has children from a previous marriage, then on the death of B, having first inherited A's share, the whole property has to be divided between A and B's current children as well as B's earlier children.

Furthermore, the device is not tax efficient. When this clause is put into effect, namely when the first deceased's half share accrues to the survivor, there are full conveyance costs of about 10% to be paid on the value of the property, (which will have increased in the meantime). This would have to be paid in cash by the survivor.

In the case of A and B being married to each other, and on the death of A, the children would normally have inherited his half share, each enjoying a tax-free allowance of 300,000 F against French death duties. Had there been a *tontine*, however, they would only be inheriting the property on the death of the second parent, and the 300,000 F allowance would be applied to the whole property value. So instead of enjoying the allowance *twice* on the inheritance of each half share, they would only benefit from it *once*.

This is why the French themselves do not like the *tontine*, but then they are not bothered with the inheritance aspect. In fact, they have their own way of coping with the problem. They usually arrange for the survivor to have a life interest *(usufruit)* in the half share inherited by the children. In this way, in addition to his or her existing half share, the life interest in the remaining half share guarantees control and occupancy of the property. This is a good alternative formula for non-French huyers who do not wish to have a *tontine*.

So in conclusion, my recommendation is that the *tontine* is not necessary unless there is a complicated family situation. But if there are complications, or if the joint purchasers are not married, then professional advice should be sought from an Anglo-French practitioner who is familiar with the problem. The local notaire in France is unlikely to understand your motives. Rutherfords Consultancy operate a advisory French will service.

If two owners are not married and the intention is for each to leave the half share to the survivor, the death duties are high. 60% of the value of the half share would be payable (see chapter on Tax for rates of death duty). A solution would be for each to insure his or her life with the proceeds going to the survivor, which would take care of the unwelcome tax payment. In fact **death duties** decrease the closer the blood ties. See chapter 9 on tax for the rates of death duties.

It is sometimes put about that by forming a **SCI** *(société civile immobilière)* all these inheritance complications can be avoided. This is a misconception, for two reasons. If you are non-resident in France, then your movable effects, including your SCI shares, escape the rules. But if you are a French resident, then *all* your assets are subject to the inheritance laws. Secondly, many British buyers erroneously think they have a problem with French inheritance. It is pointless going to the trouble and expense of forming a SCI when there may be no problem that needs solving in the first place.

The main advantages of a SCI have nothing to do with inheritance and you will find them set out in chapter 13.

13. SETTING UP IN BUSINESS

Part I

An overview

Since the late 1980s the trickle of foreigners setting up in business in France has turned to a sizeable flow, if not yet a full scale flood. This is due in part to the number of British entrepreneurs wishing to escape the recession in Britain and hoping to tap in to the growing population of settlers in France, British or otherwise. Their path has been smoothed by the Single Market rules that came into effect with the European Union.

I have to confess that I have shaken my head at the naive optimism of some of these budding businessmen, some of whom were not businessmen at all and whose efforts were doomed from the start. If faith could move mountains then the Alps would have ended up in Brittany.

It is difficult enough to start up a business at the best of times, but in a foreign country with a different legal system and an entirely alien commercial ethos, it is ..... I will refrain from saying impossible because that would be unfair. Suffice it to say that such daring is tantamount to being thrown in at the deep end of the pool with one hand tied behind your back and with a set of rules that you have not understood. The locals will surely swim past you with an impeccable crawl, splashing water in your face as they go pass. If you are still game then read on.

In those countries that the French like to call Anglo-Saxon, meaning mainly the United Kingdom and the United States, there is a freedom to trade quite unknown in Continental Europe. In Britain you can set up in business without notifying a single soul in authority. Naturally if you make a profit (in your first year? unlikely) you must impart the good news to your Inspector of Taxes. You do not even have to register for Value Added Tax until your turnover reaches a relatively high threshold.

In France, and the French are not alone in this, there is an obstacle course of great complexity to be completed before you can open for business. Some types of business are easier than others and require fewer documents and permits before you are *en règle*. It is important to understand how businesses are classified.

Whether it is your intention to become self-employed or to form a limited company, learn which category applies to you. Each activity falls into a pigeonhole that determines its structure and tax treatment. Find yourself in the wrong category and you will end up paying too much tax or even prevented from trading in the way you intended.

Businesses are broken down into the following categories:

Artisans *(activités artisanales)* which include self-employed builders, plumbers and electricians.

Trading *(activités commerciales)* including shopkeepers and all those who buy and sell for gain. Agents, brokers, campsite, hotel and restaurant owners are also included.

Professions. In France self-employed accountants, lawyers, architects, etc. are not treated as self-employed but as *professions libérales*, each with its own set of rules.

Civil activities. A private individual who lets out his property for summer rentals or who offers rooms on a bed & breakfast basis (up to maximum of 6 rooms) is undertaking *civil* and not *commercial* activity. But if he let furnished rooms all year round, then that is *commercial*. On the other hand, unfurnished tenancies offered by private landlords are treated as *civil*. I am not saying this to confuse you, but to illustrate the importance of understanding which category applies to your business. The tax implications are considerable.

Other categories include **industrial** and **agricultural**.

Taking on employees
The best advice I can give to anyone contemplating the hiring of staff in France is "avoid it if you can". There is a high degree of employee protection and the employer will find it a lot more difficult to fire than to hire. There is a plethora of official records to be kept and failure to do so can result in fines. These records include:

- A wages book *(livre de paie)* with each page stamped by the local mayor summarising your pay records. This document must contain no blanks or erasures (white correction fluid is deemed by French officials to be subversive). It must be retained for 5 years (10 years for a trading company). Penalty for non-compliance 3,000 F.

- A staff register *(registre du personnel)* listing details of all your employees. It must be retained for 5 years with effect from the last entry. Penalty for non-compliance 5,000 F.

- A register of the observations and recommendations made to you by the labour inspector on his periodic visits, mainly in respect of safety and hygiene.

- A register of staff representatives and the staff problems brought to your attention by them together with the replies given (businesses with 11 employees or more).

- Documents listing the hours worked by each employee to be made available to the labour inspector.

In addition to all this, the main disincentive to hiring staff in France is one of cost. The bane of all French managers is the high level of employer's social security contributions. In Britain the employer pays on average 10.2% over and above gross salary. In France it is a swingeing 40%[1], and this can go up to 50% for senior managers. Then there are the minimum 30 working days (5 weeks) of paid holiday, and many staff expect 2 months pay in December *(le treizième mois)* although the latter is not compulsory.

All parties agree that the high cost of employing staff in France exacerbates the unemployment problem. It is politically difficult to solve; the money for the high degree of social security in France has to come from somewhere.

[1] Whereas in Britain there is a single all-purpose employer's contribution under the heading National Insurance, in France the employer has to pay 12.8% for sickness insurance, 9.8% for the pension fund, 5.4% towards child benefit and further payments for industrial accidents, unemployment, training, etc.

Value Added Tax *(Taxe sur la valeur ajoutée)*
In Britain, businesses with an annual turnover of less than £46,000 are not obliged to register for Value Added Tax. They benefit by being able to charge their customers less, but on the other hand they cannot

claim benefit for the VAT they pay on supplies.

In France, all businesses must register for VAT *(TVA)*. There are, at the time of going to press, just two rates: 5.5% for foodstuffs, books and some equipment for the disabled, and 18.6% for all other goods and services (I have yet to discover why 18.6% and not 18.5%).

Businesses with low turnover on which annual TVA due does not exceed 5,400 F (20,000 F for artisans) benefit from special allowances that reduce the net amount payable.

Returns must be made monthly but can be made quarterly if the TVA payable does not exceed 12,000 F. Completion of the TVA return is unbelievably complicated. To give an idea, the same return in Britain consists of 9 boxes to be filled in (it used to be 5 boxes but the European Union made us increase the number). The French version comprises 96 boxes (that is for the "simplified" version, the full version has more!).

TVA returns accompanied by your cheque must never be sent in late, otherwise cash penalties are automatically imposed. On the other hand, if your inputs exceed your outputs, the tax office has to send *you* a cheque. This often happens when a business has just been launched and the volume of sales is slow to build up. In Britain the VAT refund is paid by the Customs and Excise usually within 2 weeks and certainly within the month. In France expect to wait 6 months, a delay that creates quite a strain on cash flow.

Conclusion
If after all this you are still determined to set up in business, then you can take heart from the fact that once you have the hang of the system, it all becomes much more manageable. You can also turn to a local accountancy or book-keeping firm to help you with all the forms, especially TVA returns and payslips. For a fixed annual fee, they will take care of all the routine fiscal administration. They are not expensive (some charge less in one year than some UK accountants cost *per hour*). However, they will limit themselves to the strict routine. You cannot expect them to think creatively for you nor to input the type of wide-ranging advice that a more expensive British accountant will give you.

I also have to say that although the Continental system of business is so bureaucratic and regulated, any worthwhile *entrepreneur* will take it all in his stride. After all, there are many successful businessmen in Europe who have a thing or two to say about the red tape, but consider it no real impediment to building up a successful business. Profitability is no lower abroad than at home.

Part II

Thumb nail sketches of some businesses in France
The types of business that British persons usually start up in France fall into three main categories:

- Travel orientated activities, namely hotels & restaurants, holiday rentals including *gites*, bed & breakfast, campsites, etc.
- Building trades.
- Other activities. In this category I would include shop-keeping, but also property based businesses including chateau conversions, language schools, seminar & conference centres.

Anyone wishing to embark on a **travel orientated activity** would be advised not to enter the field of **hotel-restaurants** unless they are already experienced. An actor client of mine was quite inexperienced but pressed on with the conversion of a property into a hotel-restaurant. The location was sublime, overlooking a famous river, and the overall package quite seductive - on paper at least. But as he put it when the business folded, it was "an artistic triumph but a box office disaster". The problem is that hotels and restaurants in tourist locations are easy to fill in season and at weekends out of season. What sets the successful hotelier apart from his competitors is the ability to do business on rainy weekdays in November. The bills have to be paid, whatever the weather and at all times of year. Remember too that hotels in France are licensed by the Ministry of Tourism and allocated a number of stars depending on the number and quality of facilities.

Many British owners, on the other hand, have successfully taken on a **holiday rental or bed & breakfast** operation. Although success in this field is easier to achieve, I cannot stress too much that such activities should be regarded as a source of "top-up" revenue and not as bread winners in themselves. They are indeed useful as extra income and also serve to keep someone active when in full or early retirement and to maintain human contact. As with all businesses linked to the travel

... an artistic triumph but a box office disaster ...

industry, their seasonal nature renders them sensitive to the vagaries of fluctuating demand.

First, a definition of *gîtes*. A *gite* (or more precisely a *gite rural*) is the name given to modest self-catering accommodation in a country setting that is owner-managed. Strictly speaking, to call yourself a *gite* operator you have to register with the *Gites de France* organisation, although some independent owners still call their cottages *gites*

Many buyers of French property who plan to live permanently in France are tempted by the idea of converting outbuildings into rental units and earning some income that way. It is also a good way to keep busy for part of the year if one is retired. There are *gite* complexes now on the market being sold as going concerns and this kind of purchase would allow one to start earning straightaway.

There are advantages and disadvantages in belonging to the Gites de France organisation. Some of the chief merits are *first* that you benefit from their marketing and will receive bookings without further effort on your part. The level of rent, however, will not be high but then that is the whole point of the exercise. On the other hand, your advertising expenses will be low. The *second* advantage is that you can, under certain circumstances, get a grant for the conversion of your outbuilding or further upgrading of the cottage. The grant, however, will be a proportion of what you spend yourself, so that to get a bigger grant you have to put your hand deeper in your pocket.

There are rules of course. For example, each bedroom has to measure at least 12 square metres and there has to be a properly tended garden. An inspector will come to check. For more information about Gites de France, contact them at Fédération Nationale des Gites de France, 35 rue Godot de Mauroy, 75009 Paris.

A good many persons, however, stay outside the organisation and arrange for their own marketing and advertising. This is necessary if you do not live on site, a *gite* owner being by definition a local resident. Absentee owners who have to do their own advertising end up spending more, but then can probably charge more too. Others place their properties in the hands of British travel companies specialising in French country self-catering holidays. Be sure to appoint a well established company. Alternatively, you can get your holiday unit into one of the ferry company brochures. Brittany Ferries in particular have an effective holiday programme. (They have the advantage of being able to offer their customers packages inclusive of ferry crossing). Whichever you choose, remember that in the travel business, the lead-in time is very long. To get your property into next year's brochure, you need to contact the company *one year ahead*.

Whether you join the *Gites de France* organisation or not, you will benefit from a relatively benign tax regime. Your status will be one of a private property owner renting out spare accommodation for short holiday lets. However, those owners who collect their rent in their home countries outside France have often not declared any income in France itself. Now, the rules state that the tax jurisdiction depends on where the property is located. Thus even if you sign contracts with your holiday tenants and collect their money in Britain, the income is strictly speaking taxable in France. The French tax authorities have so far not been in much of a position to levy tax on this income, but now with the huge increase in such holidays I suspect that it will not be long before the rules are tightened. Either way, you will not end up paying tax twice, thanks to the Anglo-French double tax convention.

By definition, a *gite* operator has a semi-amateur status, being a private individual who happens to rent out holiday accommodation on a seasonal basis. Those who wish to take the exercise more seriously then become **loueurs en meublé** (landlords of furnished premises that are let for short periods). Anyone who runs a holiday complex as a trade will fall into this category. This involves operating multiple units and achieving a correspondingly higher turnover. That in turn means hopefully higher profits which bring in their wake a stricter tax regime. I would strongly advise against starting off as a *loueur en meublé* unless you are already a professional at this business. Better to find your feet first as *gite* operator and take it from there.

Another favourite is to offer **bed & breakfast** *(chambres d'hôte)*. This kind of business is useful for anyone wishing to make use of spare bedrooms in their French house. As with *gites* you can earn useful income and have an activity that keeps one busy. There is a division within the Gites de France organisation called Chambres d'Hôte with whom you can register. This will bring you business and will allow you to display the Chambres d'Hôte plaque which will attract passing trade. Again, as with Gites de France, you do not have to be a member and many prefer to make their own advertising arrangements. The Hexagon magazine contains a directory of British Bed & Breakfast in France.

The tax treatment for bed & breakfast operators is also quite benign, provided you have no more than six bedrooms (with a total capacity not exceeding 15 persons) on offer to the public. Any more and you will be deemed to be running a full scale business.

If you propose to supply meals other than breakfast, then you will be operating a **guest house** *(table d'hôte)*. The number of meals offered must not exceed the capacity of the bed & breakfast, and must be served at the same time. You will require a scaled down version of a restaurant licence *(petite licence restaurant)* which is free.

Quite a few people are considering opening a new, or buying an existing, **campsite**. Let me explain a few of the general rules. All French campsites of 26 pitches or more have to be licensed by the Minsitry of Tourism and given a classification of 1 to 4 stars depending on the facilities on offer. A site of 25 pitches or less in a rural setting is called *camping à la ferme*. This is the campsite equivalent of bed & breakfast. It is regarded as a sideline activity and not as a business proper. No one ever got rich running a *camping à la ferme*.

I would advise against embarking on a campsite project unless you are already a professional in the business, for the following reasons. If you buy an existing site, you have to ask yourself why the owners are selling. If they have failed to make a profit or if they are retiring, you can assume that the campsite is "tired" and will need upgrading. This will involve extra expense. Also special efforts will have to be made to attract a clientele that is becoming more demanding. Plenty of leisure facilities must be laid on, games organised and so on. You will need to spend *at least* 2 million francs to have a campsite that will provide you with a modest living.

Some are considering buying a green field site and converting it to a campsite. This will be very difficult unless you are a professional. You must also bear in mind that many municipalities run their own sites and if you are likely to clash with one of these, you will not get your planning permission.

Part III

What type of format?
In Britain there are just two types of limited liability company - privately owned with "Ltd" after its name, and the "Plc" which has shareholders drawn from members of the public. The alternative is to trade in one's own name, either as a sole trader or as a partnership. A sole trader can start up without telling a soul. Once he is up and running, only the tax office need be notified. Partners in a partnership have a partnership agreement, not to satisfy any bureaucrats but to establish on paper the working relationship between the partners.

In France, on the other hand, trading entities come in a myriad of forms, incorporated and unincorporated, with limited liability and without. I shall limit myself to the most common ones.

- Sole trader *(entreprise individuelle)*. This is the form that I would recommend for anyone starting up in a modest way of business. True, there is no limited liability, but the sole trader in France is spared a lot of the expense and paperwork of running a company.

- *EURL (entreprise unipersonnelle à responsabilité limitée)*. This is a limited company owned by a single shareholder, and is for the sole trader who requires the protection of limited liability.

- *SARL (société à responsabilitée limitée)*. This is the equivalent of the British "Ltd" company with a minimum of two shareholders and 50,000 F capital.

- *SA (société anonyme)*. There must be at least seven shareholders and a capital of 250,000 F. This is the closest equivalent to our "Plc".

- *SCI (société civile immobilière)*. This is an incorporated partnership whose sole object is to own property. It cannot trade.

- *SNC (société en nom collectif)*. This is the standard form of trading partnership. It is not suitable for an ambitious enterprise, but can be useful if two or more partners wish to test the market before undertaking the expense of forming a SARL.

There are many others, and some professions each have their own type of incorporated partnership.

Forming a company in France is expensive. Whereas in Britain, a "Ltd" company can be bought off the shelf for about £80, in France each one has to be tailor made. The cost is about 10,000 F. This includes *all* the extras, and beware of quotations given by notaires and other practitioners who quote just their fee and omit the cost of VAT, filing fee, gazetting, and other expenses. In addition, the capital has to be paid upfront *in cash*. This is a minimum of 50,000 F for a humble SARL. Forget the English system of £100 companies with only £2 paid up. In France, the capital remains blocked in a bank account until the bank receives the certificate of incorporation (form *K bis*). Since this document can take as long as one month to procure, your precious cash will remain locked for the duration.

The registered office *(siège social)* of a French company has to be a proper trading address. It is not possible to use one's home, nor to use an accommodation address or that of an accountant.

Which type of company?

The **EURL.** Although called a "company" *(société)*, it is not one at all since there is only one shareholder. Be that as it may, this form of one-man-band has some useful advantages, namely:

- It provides the owner/manager with limited liability. Whereas a sole trader has no such protection with his personal assets, including his home, being at risk if he should fail to pay his creditors, the EURL separates the assets of the business from those of the owner. On the other hand, the owner cannot mingle the two. For example, he cannot pledge the assets of the business to support a personal liability.
- Should the owner wish to expand, he can transform his EURL into a SARL (see below) relatively easily. In this way, he can take on other shareholders and develop the business. On the other hand, a businessmen cannot be owner of more than one EURL.
- There are some inheritance advantages, and these are important to the French. For example, a sole trader cannot bequeath his business to his children. It dies with him. On the other hand, the shares of a EURL can be passed on to a successor on the owner's retirement or death.
Taxation. The company is subject to tax on its net profit at 33.33% but any drawings by the owner/manager are tax deductible. These will then be assessed as his personal income.

The **SARL**. This is the most common form of trading entity just like the British limited liability company. There must be at least two shareholders *(associés)*. However, there is no board of directors, since the company is run by a manager *(gérant)*, or if there are two of you by joint managers *(co-gérants)*. The advantages of this form of business are well known, namely:
- The assets of the company are separate from those of the shareholders, so that their risk is limited to the capital that they have contributed. (Beware of wrongful trading. The French are very strict with company directors who trade while insolvent).
- The share structure of a company gives the owners flexibility to expand by taking on new shareholders, merging or acquisitions.
- The same inheritance advantages apply as to the EURL, although with a multi-shareholder company the interests of the other shareholders have to be taken into consideration. What happens to the shares on the death of a shareholder has to be set out in the articles of association *(statuts)*.
Taxation. The company is subject to tax at 33.33% on its net profit. Again as with the EURL, the manager's pay is tax deductible, and he in turn is personally assessed.

The **SA**. Since this is the French equivalent of the British public limited company (Plc), you obviously have an ambitious project in mind and you will have deep pockets. The subject is too serious and complicated to be covered within a paragraph of a book such as this one. Your minimum investment of 250,000 F needs the protection of professional advisers before you proceed. The SA must have a board of at least three directors.

While on this subject let me bring to your attention a few common misunderstandings in the use of the word "director" in French:
- a *directeur* is not a director, but a manager (of a shop or a bank, for example),
- the manager of a SARL on the other hand is a *gérant*,
- the director of a SA is an *administrateur*.

The **SCI**. This is an incorporated partnership designed for owning property. A lot is said about this form of company, often for the wrong reasons, and I fear some legal practitioners recommend this form of property ownership because they earn a nice fee for setting the company up for you.

First of all a SCI is not permitted to trade. Its purpose is purely to own property. However, like a private individual it can let it and earn a rent from it, but it cannot buy and sell houses as a trade. Its main advantages are as follows:
- It is useful when there is multiple ownership of a property. For example, four individuals might buy a house. Each owner would then own one quarter (25%) of the shares in the company. Now if one of them wished to sell out, all he would have to do is execute a share transfer, which is a much cheaper and less complicated exercise than a full notarised property sale.
- The company is tax transparent. This means that the shareholders are all taxed as if they were private individuals and they benefit from the usual personal allowances. This applies to rental income and capital gains tax.
- Then there is the inheritance advantage, which sometimes induces British buyers to form a SCI. This matter is referred to in greater detail in Chapter 12 on French inheritance. Briefly, the shares in a SCI can be bequeathed freely and are not bound by the strict French rules of succession, providing the shareholders are not resident in France. However the SCI is not the answer to all inheritance problems.
- If the shareholders sell the property outright, all they have to do is sell their shares - it is the company that owns the property. This would entail much lower legal charges than the usual 10-12% for a conventional notarised purchase. It could make your house easier to sell.

There must be at least two shareholders and one manager (*gérant*) who is naturally usually one of the shareholders. There can even be joint managers *(co-gérants)*. The capital would normally be the equivalent of the shareholders' total investment in the property - purchase price *plus* legal costs.

As for disadvantages, the SCI , like all French companies, is relatively expensive to form, about 10,000 F all in. Also, there is the necessity of filing a return annually. Even though the company does not trade, it can earn money by way of rental. Until you get the hang of these returns, you are going to have to use a local accountant to do them for you.

14. SELLING A FRENCH PROPERTY

Finding a buyer

Sooner or later you will want to sell your French property. Either something larger, or smaller, is required, or (as is more often the case) the children grow up and no longer use it. Whatever the motive for selling, finding a buyer for property in another country is not easy for an absentee owner. Unless you are in the happy position of having a buyer lined up in advance, you will have to use an estate agent. Ideally, he should be the agent through whom you bought the property in the first place. If you decide to offer the property in the United Kingdom, this will enhance your chances of a sale. The local French agent will pick up any business that comes his way, either a French client or other European. If you also instruct a good British agent, he will offer the house direct to the British market, where the demand for French country property is strong. Rutherfords have a department that specialises in British resales.

The Notaire

It is customary to use the notaire who handled the purchase for you originally. This is because he already has the details of the previous transaction on file and can give swifter service. In rare cases, a French purchaser may insist on using his own notaire. In this case, it is customary for the two notaires to act jointly and to split their fee. In all cases the notaire's fee and other legal charges are payable by the purchaser. The vendor should have no legal charges to pay whatever.

The procedure, of course, is very much as described in the chapter on buying, only in reverse. The purchase price will be paid to the notaire who will keep it as stakeholder, pending completion. As soon as the final deed is signed, the purchaser becomes legal owner of the property. As vendor you will not receive your money until the sale has been cleared by the mortgage office of the Land Registry (*Conservation des Hypothèques*).

If you have a British purchaser, there is nothing to prevent him from paying the purchase price in sterling in this country. In this case only the legal charges have to be paid by him directly to the notaire. It would not be normal for the purchaser to pay you direct but to place the funds with a stakeholder pending completion.

Capital Gains Tax

The vendor will normally expect to make a capital gain on reselling his French property and, if he is a non-resident of France, the tax will be witheld from the purchase price by the notaire and paid over by him to the tax office. The rate is 33.33%, although there are some allowances which mitigate this. In particular, there is a generous allowance to allow for inflation. Thus, the longer the vendor has owned the property, the greater this allowance will be. Furthermore, there is a further allowance of 6,000 F that is applied automatically. Full details of French CGT are provided in the chapter on tax.

The notaire will complete the tax return, which the vendor has to sign. The tax is taken from the sale proceeds and forwarded to the tax office. In order to protect themselves against errors, the tax authorities have required that non-resident vendors appoint a guarantor who resides in France to guarantee against any shortfall in the amount of tax levied. The guarantor has to be approved in advance by the tax office and only persons of substance are acceptable. Because of the difficulty that the appointment of such guarantors can present, the vendor can sometimes apply for a dispensation. If the sale is relatively uncomplicated and the tax easy to calculate, the exemption is usually granted. If not, there are specialist firms that can provide the guarantee for a fee.

By virtue of the Anglo-French Double Tax Agreement, any capital gains tax payable in France can be offset against tax due on the same transaction in the United Kingdom.

15. EDUCATION

What will be of particular concern to readers of this book is the ease with which their own children can be introduced into the French system. A decision to start a new life in France can turn on this one issue, if school age children are involved.

Naturally, much depends on the children themselves since some are more adaptable than others. Generally the younger thay are, the easier it is for them to learn French and make new friends.

My recommendation is that you get to know a local British family that has been through the exercise. In this way, you can benefit from their experience. You will find that generally all have come out of it very well, and that the children soon acquire considerable fluency in French and end up correcting their parents' mistakes.

How it works

Schooling is compulsory between the ages of 6 and 16 for all children resident in France of whatever nationality. State education is free of charge. Private schools, mainly maintained by religious organisations, are fee paying. The right to free education is sacrosanct in France in very much the same way as the British believe in free health care.

The State education system in France has a long history and is generally considered to be excellent (although it does have its critics). The teachers are well paid and academic standards are high. The hours are longer than in Britain and children have to do more homework. On the other hand, less attention is paid to sport and other activities.

Pre-Primary Education

Pre-Primary schooling, in nursery schools known as either *écoles maternelles, jardins* or *classes enfantines,* is optional and is open to children aged 2 to 6 years. It has increased in popularity over the years and although in theory compulsory schooling does not begin until 6, in fact all children attend school at the age of 5.

Primary Education
Children enter primary school at 5,6 or 7 years of age, depending on their degree of individual development.

There is no examination marking the child's passage from primary to secondary education, except in the case of children moving from a private primary school to a secondary school, and of course applying for a grant.

Secondary Education
1. *Collèges*
At the age of 10,11,12 or even 13 - depending on their progress - children leave primary school and are admitted into secondary school colleges. There is no entrance examination; each child's primary record is forwarded to the college where he will spend the next four years.
a) The first two years (called 6th and 5th)
This is the "observation cycle" in which all pupils have twenty-four hours a week of: French, mathematics, a foreign language, history, geography, civics, experimental sciences, artistic subjects, physical education and sport.
b) The last two years (called 4th and 3rd)
This is the "orientation cycle", where all pupils have twenty-four and a half hours of lessons in the subjects listed above. This timetable is completed by two to three hours a week of compulsory study of a subject chosen from the following: Latin, Greek, second modern language, a regional language or intensive study in the first foreign language.

2. *Lycées*
Lycées take pupils after the *collège* and prepare them in three years (called 2nd, 1st and terminal) for one of the following examinations:
- *baccalauréat* of secondary education (Bac)
- *brevet de technicien* (BT)

The *baccalauréat* is roughly equivalent to the British A levels but is much broader based and includes a compulsory philosophy paper. All holders of the *Bac* have automatic entry to a French university.

Private Education
The law stipulates that education is compulsory and that the State must provide schooling, but it does not give the State the monopoly of education. Private establishments co-exist with public ones and are to be found all over France, catering for 15% of the total school population. Many were founded by religious organisations, others by various

associations, professional bodies or individuals. There are also certain British or international schools that provide their teaching in English.

17. NEW MOTORWAYS AND RAIL TRACK IN FRANCE

In Britain, any new stretch of motorway that is planned more often than not has to be fought over, and public enquiries drag on as the objectors put their case.

These matters are dealt with more summarily in France. First of all the population is much more thinly spread and there are fewer protestors. Secondly, unlike Southern Englanbd, there is no concentration of articulate middle class people who know how to give as good as they get. But most important of all, motorways are not considered as *evil* but as *beneficial*. The French like motorways.

The *autoroutes* that fan out from the Channel Tunnel at Calais are welcomed as providers of wealth to the region. No matter that they crash through a chateau here or clip a village there. It is accepted that a few sacrifices have to be made for the sake of the common good.

There is no doubt that the improved network of *autoroutes* and TGV railway lines are making France a geographically more co-ordinated country. Good lines of communication are good for the economy, and that can only be good news for the property investor.

Not only are new *autoroutes* planned in France, but the new high speed train (TGV) is no doubt flavour of the decade. This amazing train travels on fast new track enabling it to reach a speed of 300km (190 miles) per hour.

Already the TGV travels on new track from Paris to Lyon and beyond, with a new routing planned as far as Nice. It also travels westwards to Brittany and south-west to Bordeaux and on to Toulouse. Paris to Bordeaux is covered in under 3 hours. Travellers from London can take the Tunnel train as far as Lille, change trains then travel onward to the south. The Mediterranean can be reached in this way in under 7 hours.

Until now the basic lines of road and rail communication have always fanned out from Paris, as though it was inconceivable that anyone should wish to travel across country from one provincial city to another. The new thinking is that the regions should be better served and accordingly there will be new axes, for example from Clermont-Ferrand to Béziers, from Vierzon to Brive and Montauban, and then a grand transversal route Bordeaux-Clermont Ferrand-Lyon.

With a few exceptions, all French *autoroutes* are subject to tolls *(à péage)*. At peak times there can be quite a queue at the toll booths. In order to speed things up for frequent users, some *autoroutes* operate an electronic payment system enabling drivers to pass the booths without stopping *(télépéage)*. A photo-sensitive sticker is placed in the bottom left hand corner of the windscreen. This is read electronically and the subscriber's bank account automatically debited. A detailed monthly statement is provided to enable him to check the debits.

If you should be unfortunate enough to lose your ticket, you will be charged the full stretch of motorway even though you may have travelled from one junction to the next.

18. GLOSSARY OF HOUSE TERMS

English to French

attic grenier

barn grange. **Dutch** or **open barn**, hangar
wash **basin** lavabo
bath baignoire
bathroom salle de bain
beam poutre. **Small beam** poutrelle
bedroom chambre
builder maçon *(ie. bricklayer, stone mason)*

cabinet maker ébéniste
electric **cable** câble
carpenter menuisier, *(roof timbers)* charpentier
ceiling plafond
cement ciment
cellar cave *(often at ground level)*
WC **cistern** chasse d'eau
concrete beton
cooker cuisinière. **Gas cooker** cuisinière à gaz

dormer window lucarne
drain égout. **Main drain** tout-à-l'égout

eave avant-toit
electrician électricien
electricity éléctricité, courant
Electricity Board E.D.F. (Electricité de France)

wooden **floor** plancher
cement **floor** sol

bottled **gas** gaz en bouteille
Butane **gas** gaz butane
Propane **gas** gaz propane
mains **gas** gaz de ville
Gas Board G.D.F. (Gaz de France)

hallway entrée
heating chauffage.
central **heating (oil fired)** chauffage central (au mazout)
immersion water **heater** cumulus
électrique

joiner menuisier
joist solive

kitchen cuisine

landing (stairs) palier
electricity/water **meter** compteur
mortar mortier

panelling *(tongue & groove on ceiling)* lambris, *(wainscotting)* boiserie
partition cloison
pipe tuyau. Ground level **pipe work** canalisation
plaster plâtre
electric **plug** fiche électrique
plasterer plâtrier
plumber plombier
electric power **point** prise de courant

refrigerator réfrigérateur
cement **rendering** crépi
plaster **rendering** enduit
roof toit. **Roofing** toiture
roof timbers charpente
room pièce
dining **room** salle à manger
drawing **room** salon
living **room** salle de séjour

shower douche
shutter *(wooden)* volet, *(on modern buildings, usually of the roll up type)* contre-vent, *(in Southern France)* persienne
septic tank fosse septique
soak away puits perdu
spring source
electric **switch** interrupteur
staircase escalier
step (stair) marche (d'escalier)

water **tank** réservoir. **Rain water tank** citerne
tap robinet
floor **tiles** carreaux. **Roof tiler** couvreur
roof **timbers** charpente

wall mur
wash basin lavabo
water eau

French to English

are 100 square metres
atelier workshop
appentis lean-to

bastide square or fortified stone house
bois woodland
bosquet small wood, spinney
buanderie wash house, laundry room

cave cellar, store room (*often at ground floor level*)
cave voûtée vaulted cellar
chai wine cellar, vat room
cheminée *not a chimney but a* fireplace
château country mansion (*except in wine growing areas, where any house no matter how humble and giving its name to a vineyard can be called a château*)
chartreuse (*in some parts of France*) a manor house
chaumière thatched cottage
colombage half timbered (house)
colombier pigeon house, dovecote
comble loft
corps de bâtiment cluster of buildings
cour yard, farmyard

débarras box room, small store room
demeure dwelling, *but usually meaning an* imposing country house
dépendances outbuildings
duplex apartment on two floors, maisonette

écurie stable
étable cowshed

forêt forest *but usually a* wood
four à pain bakehouse

garrigue scrub on Mediterranean hillside
gentilhommière small manorhouse
grange barn
gros oeuvre basic structure, shell of a house

hangar open sided barn *usually metallic*

hectare 10,000 square metres, 2½ acres

immeuble apartment block, (*legal*) immovable property

jardin garden, *usually a cultivated vegetable garden not one with lawn or borders*

logis (*in some parts of France*) a manor house

manoir manor house
maison bourgeoise period house *originally designed for the professional classes of the Edwardian or between-wars period, rather stylized and dated in appearance*
maison de campagne *not a country house but a* house in the country
mas Provençal house *nowadays extended to mean any house built in Mediterranean style*
mazet small stone hut
mètre carré square metre
mur mitoyen party wall

parc grounds of a mansion
pavillon lightly built cottage, small house
perron covered porch (*usually reached by an outside staircase*)
pierre du pays local stone
pigeonnier pigeon tower
piscine swimming pool
potager kitchen garden
prairie large meadow
pré meadow

réduit box room

souillarde scullery
surface habitable habitable surface area (*usually excluding balcony, terrace, store room, cellar, etc*)

taillis copse
talus embankment
terrain land
torchis wattle and daub

verger orchard
villa (T2,T3) modern house with garden (with 2,3 rooms + kitchen and bathroom)

19. GLOSSARY OF LEGAL TERMS

French to English

abbatement allowance (against tax) **représentant accrédité** fiscal guarantor
acompte deposit
achat purchase
acquéreur purchaser
acquisition purchase
acte de décès death certificate
acte de donation deed of gift
acte de mariage marriage certificate
acte de naissance birth certificate
acte de vente conveyance document
adjudication auction
alignement (arrêté de) road widening (directive)
apport personnel personal contribution (towards a mortgage)
arrhes deposit (refundable)
acte **authentique** notarised deed
avocat barrister, [US] attorney

bail lease
bailleur lessor

cadastre land registry
caution guarantee, security deposit
cession transfer (of property, shares, etc)
compromis de vente preliminary contract
comptant payment in cash (without a loan)
conjoint spouse
contrat contract
convention agreement
copropriété co-ownership (of property), [US] condominium
créancier creditor

dépôt de garantie deposit
domicile élu address for serving documents
droits d'enregistrement stamp duty, registration tax, transfer tax
emprunt loan
emprunter to borrow
vente aux **enchères** sale by auction
étude notaire's practice, office

impôt **foncier** local property tax
frais d'acte legal charges of deed

habitation dwelling
taxe d'**habitation** occupant's local property tax
huissier bailiff, [US] marshal
hypothèque mortgage

immeuble immovable property
impôt tax
indivis tenancy in common
inscription registered charge

jouissance possession, tenure
entrer en **jouissance** take possession

location tenancy
loyer rent

mainlevée release (of mortgage)
mandat mandate
mandataire proxy, representative
mobilier furniture

nantissement collateral security
notaire notary

paraphe initial
état **parasitaire** parasitological report, woodworm survey
plus-value capital gain
pouvoir power of attorney
prêt loan
privilège lien, preferential claim
procuration power of attorney
projet d'acte draft conveyance deed
promesse de vente undertaking to sell, preliminary contract
propriétaire owner
publicité foncière registering of title

régularisation completion of sale
représentant accrédité guarantor (for capital gains tax purposes)

servitude easement
sous-seing preliminary contract

usufruit life interest (in a property)

English to French

agreement convention
tax allowance abattement
auction (vente) aux enchères, par adjudication

bailiff huissier
bank transfer virement
barrister avocat
birth certificate acte de naissance
to borrow emprunter

capital gain plus-value
cash payment paiement au comptant
condominium copropriété
contract contrat
conveyance mutation, cession
conveyance document acte de vente
co-ownership copropriété
creditor créancier
completion régularisation

death certificate acte de décès
deposit acompte, dépôt de garantie, arrhes
notarised deed acte authentique
draft projet
draft conveyance document projet d'acte
dwelling habitation

easement servitude

freehold pleine propriété
furniture mobilier

gift donation
guarantee caution
capital gains tax impôt sur la plus-value
capital gains tax guarantor représentant accrédité

immovable property immeuble, biens immobiliers
initial paraphe
to initial (a document) parapher

joint owner copropriétaire
joint ownership copropriété [not to be confused with tenancy in common]

land terrain
land registry cadastre
landlord propriétaire

lease bail
legal charges frais d'acte
to lend prêter
lessor bailleur
to let louer
lien privilège
life interest usufruit
loan emprunt [borrow], prêt [lend]

sales mandate mandat de vente
marriage certificate acte de mariage
mortgage hypothèque
movable property meuble, biens mobiliers

notary notaire
notarised deed acte authentique
notary's office, practice étude

owner propriétaire

power of attorney procuration, pouvoir
preliminary contract compromis de vente
purchaser acquéreur
possession jouissance
vacant possession jouissance libre
proxy mandataire

receipt quittance
rent loyer
to rent louer
registered charge inscription
registration tax droits d'enregistrement

sale vente planning
search certificat d'urbanisme
spouse conjoint
stamp duty droits d'enregistrement
survey expertise
land surveyor géomètre

tax impôt
local property tax impôt foncier, taxe d'habitation
tenancy location
tenancy in common indivis
tenant locataire

vacant possession jouissance libre
valuation expertise

wealth tax impôt de solidarité sur la fortune

AVERAGE RAIN FALL IN MILLIMETRES - JANUARY

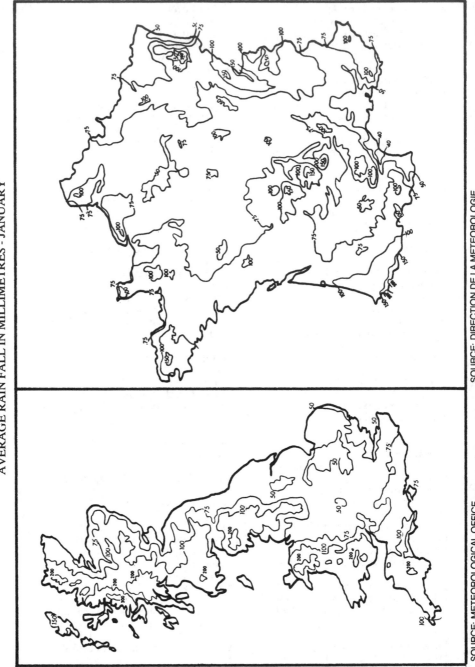

SOURCE: METEOROLOGICAL OFFICE

SOURCE: DIRECTION DE LA METEOROLOGIE

AVERAGE RAIN FALL IN MILLIMETRES - JULY

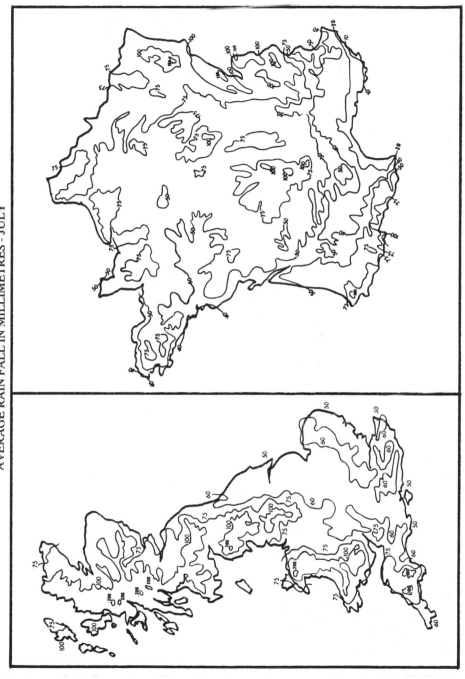

AVERAGE DAILY DURATION OF BRIGHT SUNSHINE - JANUARY

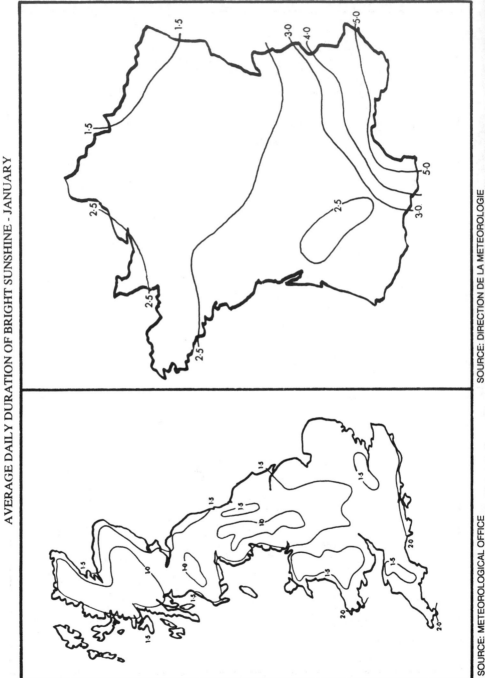

SOURCE: METEOROLOGICAL OFFICE

SOURCE: DIRECTION DE LA METEOROLOGIE

AVERAGE DAILY DURATION OF BRIGHT SUNSHINE - JULY

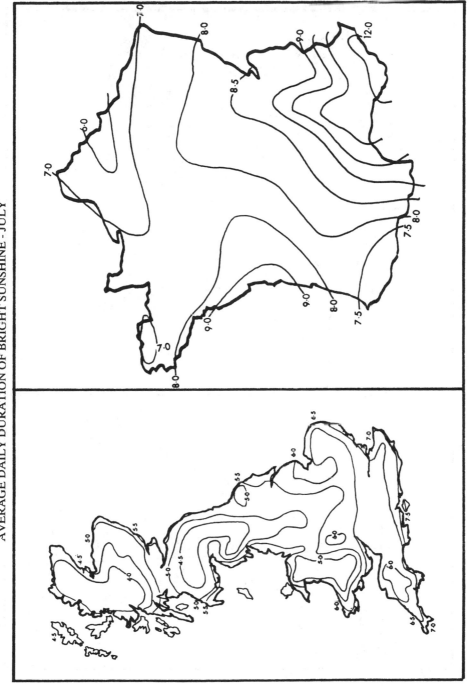

MEAN DAILY TEMPERATURE IN °C - JANUARY

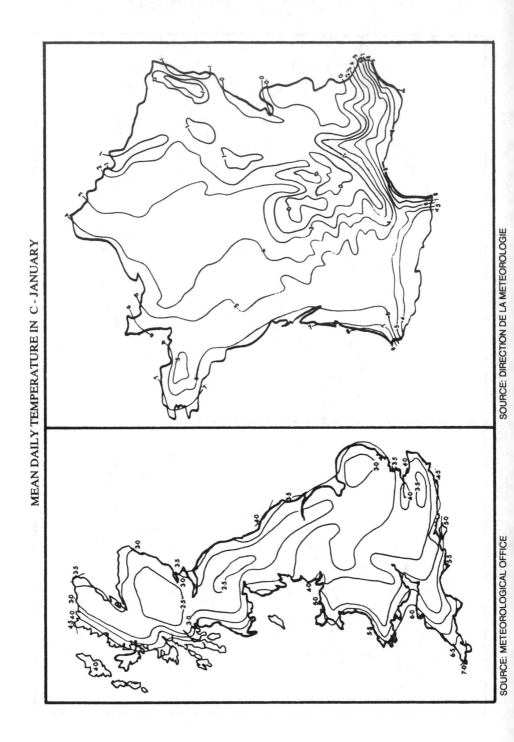

SOURCE: METEOROLOGICAL OFFICE

SOURCE: DIRECTION DE LA METEOROLOGIE

MEAN DAILY TEMPERATURE IN C - JULY

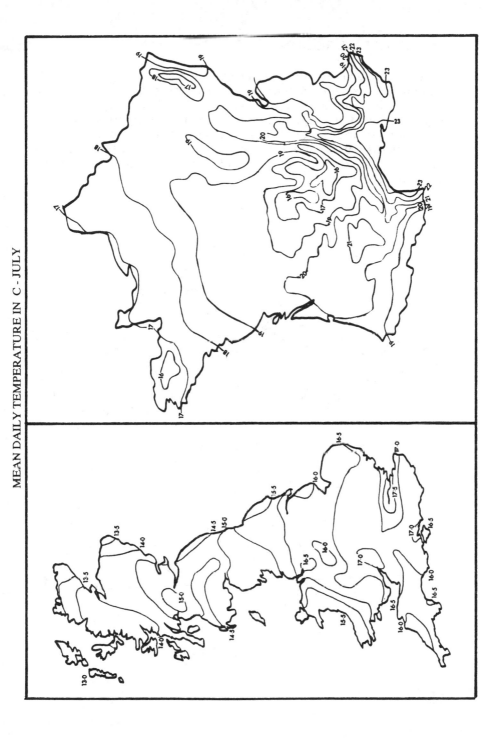

THE HISTORICAL REGIONS

The French attach much importance to the historical regions, which do not match the names of the *départements*. Hence, one can often hear the name *Périgord* instead of *Dordogne*. The larger regions were originally dukedoms (eg. Brittany, Normandy, Burgundy). Others were counties and minor fiefdoms. Usage of this nomenclature is abetted by the tourism industry which appreciates how these historic names are associated in people's minds with the romantic past. They also sound good on menus.

22. THE GREAT FRENCH PAPERCHASE

When you buy your French property, you will be asked to provide documents that will probably have lingered untouched amongst your papers for years - birth certificate, marriage certificate and, if you are divorced, a copy of the decree absolute.

Of course you will not consider this an onerous task and you will cheerfully supply copies of these documents and write it down to the experience of buying a house in France.

But wait, provision of these papers will be just the beginning of a paper chase that will last as long as you continue to conduct any affairs in France. If you have read the chapter on taking up permanent residence in France, you will begin to see the problem.

Every activity is affected. If you were to undertake the simple purchase of a butane gas bottle (essential, if you are in the countryside) you will be asked to provide your date of birth and your wife's maiden name!

Now, I have not given my date of birth to anyone in England for over twenty years. When I was asked to do so in France, frequently, my reaction at first was to say *cela ne vous regarde pas* (it is none of your business). This was received with horror. I have now given up making such observations that to me were eminently sensible but were considered at best fatuous and at worst unconstitutional.

The rub is that if a society is so steeped in the pointless shuffling of useless information and the paperwork to support it, there are vested interests that ensure the merry-go-round goes on and on.

It is a metter of how we see each other and the trust we place in our fellow beings. In England there is nothing to prevent one from buying a property, or a gas bottle for that matter, in an assumed name. Only if the motive is fraudulent does the matter of legal infringement come into it. In France the paper chase is designed to determine the legality of actions irrespective of motives, and it has become a sacrosanct ritual for its own sake.

Of course, the French do not take it lying down. They grumble about their red tape constantly, but the tape comes from a long reel dating back to Napoleon's brilliantly efficient structuring of the Empire. There is no way the tape can be unravelled now.

RUTHERFORDS
CONSULTANCY
CABINET - CONSEIL

If you feel your interests
need protecting in the realm
of Anglo-French property,
RUTHERFORDS
CONSULTANCY
will act on your behalf.

* Purchasing
* Selling
* Troubleshooting
* Inheritance advice
* Interpreting official papers
* Avoiding disputes and litigation

Plus a new service for persons applying to import their furniture & effects into France free of duty.

* Speedy provision of the appropriate application forms

* Advice on procedure and completion of forms.

* Help in the timing of the application to allow for completion of formalities.

Please apply for prospectus from:

RUTHERFORDS CONSULTANCY

25 Vanston Place
London SW6 1AZ
Tel. 0171 386 7240